A Second Chance at Life

Charlotte Ford

ISBN: 9798867073046

Go Get It Publishing, LLC
Tuscaloosa, Alabama

Dedication

With unwavering passion, I dedicate this book to my three cherished heartbeats: Kenneshia, John, and Joshua. It is God alone who deserves all the glory and honor, but through each of you, He extended His boundless love to me. We often hear children express their desire for their parents to be proud of them, but as a mother, one of my deepest aspirations has always been for each of you to be proud of me.

While I stand as the author of this book, you have all walked this incredible journey with me. Each of you has witnessed me in various stages of life, and my fervent wish is that every phase of my existence inspires you to become the best version of yourselves and to trust in God even more. You have been there for my transformation from a state of survival mode to a life overflowing with freedom, victory, and love.

John and Joshua, your presence makes being a mother to young men an exquisite experience, as you consistently demonstrate honor, love, and protection. Kenneshia, you made me a mother first and a teenage mother at that. You are an exceptional young lady, and I am profoundly grateful that you never gave up on me. You saw the Queen in me and passionately poured your prayers and unwavering efforts, urging me to acknowledge the strength and grace you envisioned. The seeds of prayer, provision, protection, and guidance I sowed into each of you have borne fruit, and I hold great admiration for you all. When you read a copy of this book, I hope you see how far "we" have come. I couldn't have asked God for better children; you infuse my life with purpose and meaning.

I cannot overlook my granddaughter, Kennedi, it is because of you that Chapter 6, "You Don't Need Permission to Live," exists. I still remember the day you whispered those words in my ear when you were just eight years old, and that moment sparked the creation of this book. You are remarkable and exceptional with a heart of gold, and I am profoundly grateful for your love and honor.

May my journey be an enduring memory for each of you, serving as a testament to God's boundless love, grace, and mercy for His children. I forever believe in you, and most importantly, I am constantly lifting you up in prayer. My love for each of you knows no bounds, and I pray that you will always love and be proud of me. I love you!

Preface

Within these pages, you will discover my journey of being granted a second lease on life. I aim to offer principles, wisdom, and guidance that can assist you in obtaining and embracing the life God has destined for you. I was finally ready and able to say I was broken and wanted to be fixed. I had a void and wanted it to be filled. I had pains that needed to be healed. Every part of me was ready. I could no longer care what others would think about me. There was a light that began to shine brightly in me. There was a resilience glowing within me, there was an outpouring of God's grace and revelation that was leading me to the still waters and green pastures. I concluded that I mattered and that I was enough. My life commenced a transformation with profound significance and purpose. Expressing in words the multitude of experiences I've undergone and triumphed over throughout the years has proven to be a monumental endeavor. This book would not be worth its "salt" without the proper words. Words are powerful, instructional, directional, measurable, and life-changing. The Word of God tells us in *John 6:63 (NLT) "The spirit alone gives eternal life. Human effort accomplishes nothing. And the very words I have spoken to you are spirit and life."* This scripture can concur with what Pierre Teilhard de Chardin stated – "We are not human beings having a spiritual experience, but we are spiritual having a human experience."

A SECOND CHANCE AT LIFE

This experience has required me to ask myself some tough questions about choices…the choices I made and why. Taking a deep dive into your soul can be frightening and life-changing at the same time. Your weaknesses, co-dependencies, lack of accountability, immaturity, and bad choices all stare you in the face and you must make another CHOICE that this is not the end but the BEGINNING!

Let me share a brief story with you: I recall the time my brother returned home after spending most of his life incarcerated, a consequence of theft driven by his struggle with drug addiction. By the time he was being released from prison, he had many medical problems. Upon his release, he displayed an unwavering aversion to idleness. Restlessness fueled his desire for constant movement, a craving to explore and savor every experience.

He would often say, "Charlotte, come on, let's grab a hamburger." In response, I would offer to take him, but decline ordering anything for myself, explaining that it was too late for me to eat, as I didn't want to gain weight. He'd gently retort, "Girl, it's only 6:00 p.m., you can indulge in a hamburger." Sometimes, he'd suggest we go for a ride, and I'd caution that we couldn't stay away for too long because I needed to return home to study. At the time, I was working towards my undergraduate degree. Regardless of his requests, I always seemed to have conditions. One day, he looked at me and said, "I thought I was the one in prison. You're living with too many restrictions and fears; that's no way to live. It's like death." My brother died less than 2 years after he was released from prison. A decade after his death, he came to me in a dream and said, "You are still living life with too many restrictions". But it wasn't just him; my other brother, who had passed away before him, both of them gazed at me. Upon awakening, my first words were an affirmation to the divine, "God, I choose life!" It is my utmost desire that you choose life! Fill your deepest desires and awaken to the most amazing and fulfilled life. You are phenomenal and I hope you know it. Your soul has a journey and it's time to begin it.

This book was destined to be the preview of a new life for me. There were some things I was praying and believing for, and God put on my heart that they would come after this book was birthed. Some things are better produced out of pain. Oftentimes when the pain no longer exists, one will downplay the phenomenon. Like the process of making wine, it cannot be produced without the crushing of grapes. The creation of this book requires the pressing of my soul and spirit. Consequently, I must pen this book as I step into the forthcoming phase of my life. Even though I am being squeezed, you all are receiving the best part of me. I'm being squeezed but I'm not bitter, I'm better. It is my prayer that the wisdom from this book will counterattack every lying word the enemy told you, the situation told you, and what you told yourself. Every chapter will introduce a practical usage coupled with a spiritual significance.

Writing this book would mean revealing parts of myself and

I was not prepared for that level of exposure. At times, I lacked the emotional, mental, and physical strength to undertake this endeavor. However, I knew one day that I was going to die, not because I was sick but because death is a part of life. I understood that if I were to pass away before completing this book, I would depart with a profound sense of unfulfillment. I would inadvertently deprive many of the invaluable wisdom and transformation that this book will impart to their lives, their families, and the generations to come.

CONTENTS

Introduction

A woman in harmony with her spirit is like a river flowing. She goes where she will without pretense and arrives at her destination, prepared to be herself and only herself.

-Maya Angelou

Regardless of the purpose, paths, and journeys we traverse to find a second chance at life, there's an undeniable truth: if you are fortunate enough to obtain it, seize it with unwavering commitment. This opportunity deserves your complete dedication, encompassing your presence, strength, passion, courage, and faith in God. You are indebted to it in every way imaginable. You've not only triumphed against insurmountable odds but also conquered adversities that aimed to dismantle you and crush your spirit. This transformation speaks to the resilience of the human spirit and the profound renewal that faith and grace can bring.

The word of God declares in *I John 4:18 that perfect love casts out all fear.* As I perfected my love for God, fear began to leave. I began to maximize the promises and principles God gave me and minimized the opinions of others. I was learning to denounce curses that others had spoken over me. If we are fearing in an area, it is because we have believed the lie of the devil that God does not love us and will not fulfill His promises in our lives.

Life follows a predetermined path, driven by the notion of

being chosen and called. This essentially matches the unique plan designed for each person by God. The attribution can be ascribed to the elements of time and chance, as highlighted in *Ecclesiastes 3*, which emphasizes the existence of a suitable time for every purpose. It does not mean that it might happen, it means that it will happen in the predestined season but still within the borders of your designated time on earth. Divine intervention will alter human-made paths to lead you into your appointed period. You hold a pivotal role in this season. You embody the spirit of Esther, summoned to the kingdom for a moment like this, possessing a resolute mindset that even in the face of potential adversity, you're resolute in seeking your purpose. *Esther 4:14-16: "For if thou altogether holdest thy peace at this time, then shall there enlargement and deliverance arise to the Jews from another place; but thou and thy father's house shall be destroyed: and who knoweth whether thou art come to the kingdom for such a time as this? 15 Then Esther bade them return Mordecai this answer, 16 Go, gather together all the Jews that are present in Shushan, and fast ye for me, and neither eat nor drink three days, night or day: I also and my maidens will fast likewise; and so will I go in unto the king, which is not according to the law: and if I perish, I perish."*

God spoke to me one day and said: "I have so many new things ready for you but the old you cannot contain them". *Luke 5:36-38 36 Then Jesus gave them this illustration: "No one tears a piece of cloth from a new garment and uses it to patch an old garment. For then the new garment would be ruined, and the new patch wouldn't even match the old garment. 37 "And no one puts new wine into old wineskins. For the new wine would burst the wineskins, spilling the wine and ruining the skins. 38 New wine must be stored in new wineskins.* The only way for me to receive this new wine would be to fully awaken and surrender to God. God was calling me to an alignment of His original purpose and plan for my life. God was calling me to a Kairos, it was time for the new wine. He was calling me out of the only life I knew, the one where I sought permission from others to live. I had to choose freedom over the validation of others. God spoke to me through *Luke 24:5 "Why do you seek the living among the dead"*. God was orchestrating a transformation in the very place where people had abandoned me, leaving me for dead. In this desolate space, God brought about a resurrection, rolling away the stones that had entombed me and awakening me to a brand-new life. What I had been searching for resided within me all along.

All the pain, suffering, and rejection have given birth to something so great in me. Pain indeed leaves a gift. One of the deeply moving aspects of pain is its ability to compel you to recognize a reservoir of strength you never fathomed within yourself. There was a void in me and layers of untapped potential. Irrespective of the diverse seasons life ushered in, be it the solitude of singlehood or the togetherness of marriage, amidst the heights of happiness or the depths of sorrow, the void within me would intermittently make its presence felt, stirring a cascade of emotions.

I could vaguely hear whispers within my spirit that there was more to life, more to me. I would almost rebuke myself when I would hear this. In the recesses of my heart, I dared myself to embrace the belief that life held untapped depths yet to be discovered. How dare I not be grateful for the life I have, regardless of the hurt and dysfunction in it? It was never a question of gratitude, but it was God calling me into alignment with His original plan for my life. I permitted my fears, the influence of others, and religious constraints to create sound barriers and blinders that prevented me from perceiving or understanding the path that God had laid out for my life. The divine intentions that God held for my life began to pose a threat to others, as they could no longer exploit or gain from my state of naivety and brokenness. This caused the warfare to intensify, underscoring the profound shift taking place. Demonic strategies that captivated me in repetitive, unfruitful seasons and cycles were being exposed and annihilated through revelation and wisdom of God's word and my kingdom assignment.

My purest and deepest desire for a second chance at life became my greatest struggle. Once more, God was initiating a reset, inviting me towards a beautiful beginning, an opportunity to step into the life He had originally designed for me. This time I could visualize it, but there were still struggles in me and the head of it was fear. God illuminated the truth that I could no longer remain a mere bystander in my breakthrough; I was called to be an active participant, engaging fully and wholeheartedly. Whenever the concept of self-worth eludes your comprehension, you inadvertently become the architect of your downfall, undermining every positive opportunity that comes your way. I did not want to do what it would take for God's plans to manifest in my life. This necessitated a departure from the familiar, shedding the skin of the old life, and embracing the emergence of a new existence. However, God had awakened me to purpose, and it was undeniable. It was a life aligned with God; it was a choice. God spoke this to me: "I will not put it in your lap, but I will put it in your reach." *James 2:26 KJV For as the body without the spirit is dead, so faith without works is dead also.* I knew I had to partner with God to live the predestined life of purpose, destiny, and happiness that He desired for me.

Numerous individuals spend their lives within one of two realms: the Past or the Future. They yearn for what has been, struggle to let go or hasten for a brighter future to come. Nevertheless, there exists a crucial space that demands recognition – the Present. Faith is not ignoring what is, but acknowledging what is and seeing the possibilities of what will be. However, the problem can be your foundation, which is a lack of understanding the Kingdom of God and understanding of the original purpose of man. To know a product but lack understanding of the creative purpose of that product still puts you at a disadvantage. *Proverbs 4:7 KJV "Wisdom is the principal thing; therefore, get wisdom: and with all thy getting get understanding."* Joshua and Caleb trusted God's plan and they walked away with the victory (*Numbers 14*). They believed and walked in God's plan without delay, having no fear of the giants, and received the blessing. Their faith and trust in God allowed them to enter into the Promised Land. *Numbers 26:65 For the Lord had said of them, "They will all die in the wilderness."* Not one of them survived except Caleb son of Jephunneh and Joshua son of Nun.

It's possible that while you have faith in God's overarching plan, you may struggle to align with the idea that the present moment is ripe for His plan to materialize in your life. You can see it happening for others but not yourself. When I earlier expressed that God had stirred me to a sense of purpose. Not only did He ignite that purpose within me, but He also unveiled a sense of eternity. He clarified my purpose and emphasized that the time for its fulfillment was now. I want you to know that it is also your time. God is awakening you to purpose and eternity, your next is now.

God brought me to the season of NOW. Just as God awakened me to destiny, he also awakened me to eternity. Let me explain. He knows your frailty, your death date, the date that if you knew what it was, you would live life according to his Kingdom plans and become who God called you to be without hesitation. One of the biggest deceptions in the world is that most people believe they have time, underestimating the gift of time and chance. The timing of your death is not a random occurrence or a result of chance. The Bible makes it clear that this is in the hands of God. God is very intentional about our living and time of death. *Job 14:5 NIV - "A person's days are determined; you have decreed the number of his months and have set limits he cannot exceed."* God pulled me into isolation to let me know my clock was ticking and I was losing the sense of time and chance. My intention is not to redirect your attention to physical death but rather to encourage you to center your focus on fully experiencing the God-given life before its earthly conclusion.

God was inviting me to a greater relationship with Him and not a religion. When one is in a race, when there is a false start, the race is immediately stopped, and the runners must start again. The whistle blows, the flags are thrown, and there is a sound that is made to let you know to stop and go back to the starting line. Many people ignore the call to return, so they keep running. Just as in sports, false starts can result in penalties and disqualifications. Now because you've gone so far, the thought of starting again seems impossible. Your mind might be fixated on the notion of starting over, yet God is allowing us to start a new journey. To start right with God is a game changer. *Zechariah 1:3 "Return to me and I will return to you".* When you return to God, it puts you in a prophetic position. You are now on the winning team, no matter what time you show up. *Matthew 19:1-16* speaks of a parable that summarizes God's unmerited favor and authority. God can move you forward, favor you, bless you according to His will, and reward you greatly, regardless of how long you've been trying. He can orchestrate remarkable leaps, altering the very course of your journey. His modus operandi transcends the confines of worldly conventions and earthly norms. *The earth is the Lord's and the fullness thereof (Psalms 24).* When He calls you, run to Him. You are thinking about what you will lose, have to reaccumulate, and have to give up. It is important to understand that some losses are gains. We've been trained to think the worst, which is a trick and deception of the enemy. The enemy knows if he can keep you in fear, you will never move forward. Navigating through life, it is all too common to gradually lose sight of your purpose, a phenomenon that transcends gender. After many years of nurturing, supporting, loving, caring, and motivating others, you realize that you lost yourself. An even greater question is how do you find yourself? Do you even have the strength to embrace life for yourself? You fought for everyone else, you suffered in silence, now do you have enough courage to dream again? You ask yourself, is it even worth it? I hope your answer is a resounding Yes, Yes, Yes and Yes! God created you for greatness. You have been mismanaged by others, do not mismanage yourself. You may feel like your season has passed you by, but I want you to know that you are right on schedule. You are wiser, smarter, stronger, and better. You must believe in yourself. You must believe in God. You must believe in the original plan God has for your life. Promises are awaiting you. It's time to live!

Chapter 1 – It's Time to Dig Deep and Uncover

We cannot expect to change what's in the world unless we first awaken what lies deeply within. - Dr. Terarai Trent

As you delve into this chapter, let the word "UNCOVER" resonate within you. Take this journey with me, be honest and truthful, this is required to get to the next level of your life. As you look back at things that happened in your past or upbringing, it will allow you to uncover patterns, cycles, and even generational curses that you never knew existed. You will start to uncover, then discover, and ultimately recover everything due you. The foundation of my upbringing would embed itself in my existence; it wasn't until years later that I began to grasp how profoundly it shaped my behaviors, choices, convictions, and mental framework. Out of roots, branches emerge. You give birth to the seeds planted in you. Certain seeds within you remain hidden until they blossom in full view. *Luke 6:43 NLT A good tree can't produce bad fruit, and a bad tree can't produce good fruit.* The seed will determine the type of fruit it will bear. If you do not like the fruit on the tree, it is time to dig deep, uncover and uproot. As you begin to uncover, the things that God reveals to you will propel you to a place of discovery and recovery. The hidden things will be revealed. You will begin to seek God more intensively. *Jeremiah 33:3* will take you by storm - *"Call to me and I will answer you and tell you great and unsearchable things you do not know"*. A revelation will occur, exposing generational curses, entrenched traditions, witchcraft, deceptive masks stemming from religious misconceptions, and false doctrines that have taken root in churches, educational systems, cultures, societies, governments, families, and within yourself.

This chapter could have been titled "Reflections". It will identify what mirrors and shadows you have been viewing yourself from. It will help you identify if you are walking around with someone else's identity. Are you a case of mistaken identity? Whose driver's license is in your wallet? Whose lies are you carrying? Whose fears are you carrying? Is your depression chemical or situational? Whose sickness have you become one with? Whose brokenness are you carrying? Perhaps it was friendly fire that killed your soul, dreams, hopes, and ambitions. Have you been sleeping with the enemy? When you begin to ask these questions, you become aware that something is missing…that something is not right. You realize that realignment needs to take place. Aware that there is more to life. Aware that you have been mismanaged. You are awakening to both the physical and spiritual environment around you, and your fervor to comprehend your God-given life is intensifying. This is a good thing; it means you have awakened. Some people never wake up, they die in an illusion. They die in fear. They die in brokenness. Sadly, some even die by taking their lives into their own hands, by suicide. They never discovered who they were. They never got restoration and restitution on this side. Perhaps they died with dreams, with creativity, with things they planned to do but kept putting it off. Dr. Myles Munroe probably said it best: "Perhaps the graveyard is one of the wealthiest places." Full of poems we will never get a chance to hear, full of exquisite art we will never get a chance to see, full of the most heartfelt, soulful music we will never get a chance to hear, full of singing that sounds like a heavenly choir, full of ground-breaking cures for diseases and illnesses, full of smiles that could light up an auditorium, full of jokes that can cause you to laugh hurts and pain away, full of so much life that was never lived. If you are reading this book, that means you still have time to uncover, discover, and recover.

There's a wealth of discovery and revelation within you, with numerous layers yet to be revealed. The unmasking must take place for you to understand and align yourself with the original plan of God. You possess a divine identity bestowed upon you by

God, one that the devil is determined to keep hidden from you. The devil reaches at you early in life, to stain, wound, and hurt you in ways that cause you to be bitter with life and God. Through relentless attempts, the adversary will endeavor to make you believe that you are flawed merchandise. Remember the devil's greatest and most powerful weapon is deception. Demonic structures were established to ensure your downfall, yet fundamental principles were established to secure your triumph. Spirits are vying for your attention, spirits of good and evil.

Uncovering and digging deep can be very painful but it is necessary. You stare at things face to face that you wish you could make disappear, you cringe because you know this will take work, and it will cause you to deny what others think about you. It will cause you to wonder if living your best life is worth it, if there's even such a thing. You will face instances of self-sabotage; occasionally distancing yourself from individuals who genuinely care about you and desire nothing more than to witness your liberation and prosperity. You'll find yourself saying, "I shouldn't complain; God has truly showered me with blessings." However, the emotions you're experiencing have nothing to do with your gratitude towards God. It's about crafting an inaccurate story. There is always a reason behind the decisions you make. To skip over them, you may say I do not know why I made that decision. Digging deep afforded me the opportunity and revelation to understand why I made certain decisions. Accepting the opportunity of a second chance at life can be painful but it is worth it. Imagine gazing out of the window, filled with desires and aspirations, but then contemplating the sacrifices required to attain them, the price to be paid. In such moments, you may opt to persist in suffering and deprivation instead. I pondered over how others would perceive me, what judgments they might pass, and whether I could truly endure this, fully aware of the distress and pain I was grappling with. What if I take a step ahead and find myself facing even more dire circumstances? All these thoughts were racing through my mind as I observed the state of the world and economy. Your mental psychological state will go haywire. Your emotional navigational system will continue to lose signal because you are traveling to a place where natural logic is not sustainable. You are going to a place, a season that you do not have an address to, it is not a location, it's a new life. So, every time you try to put it in a location, there is no signal for it. In some cases, you must set sail without a map. *I Corinthians 2:9 KJV - "But as it is written, Eye hath not seen, nor ear heard, neither have entered into the heart of man, the things which God hath prepared for them that love him."* Your inherent navigation system continuously signals "re-routing, re-routing." Those natural navigational systems cannot appropriately lead you in this season. *Proverbs 3:5-6. Trust in the Lord with all thine heart and lean not to your own understanding but in all your ways acknowledge Him and He will direct thy paths.* The more you trust God and seek Him, you will understand His leading. He will make your path plain and will guide you safely into this new season. Always keep a pure heart. This is a move of God. Only you know what you buried and why. Some things you buried need to stay buried but if you buried yourself with it, your dreams, your plans, your hopes, your purpose, your happiness, your destiny; then you have a problem. You continue to put purpose & destiny on hold because it is too painful to uncover the hidden things that are holding you back. *Hosea 4:6 KJV - "My people are destroyed for a lack of knowledge."* The process of uncovering is where you identify evil and hidden agendas, and remove its grip of power from your life. It is where you flip the script. You begin to see that the thing, issue, or person has lost its control over you, it is no longer a stronghold. You want someone to go with you, hold your hand, and take the journey with you. You are looking for someone else to do it first. The person you are looking for is yourself. We are a success story. We are the individuals God chose to break generational curses. We are the ones God brought out of darkness to His marvelous light. We are citizens of the Kingdom of God. The longer you wait, the harder it will be. As time passes, roots grow deeper and stronger. You notice that by lifting from this point, a cascade of other elements begins to unravel. Hence, you opt to remain within this situation, choosing mere survival. To mend the pain, you engage in activities such as taking vacations, acquiring assets like a house or car, setting additional objectives, immersing yourself in work, dedicating yourself to religious activities, seeking joy from going to church and centering your life around your children. At some point, none of those things will be enough to hold you. Similar to a hungry baby repeatedly rejecting a pacifier, their yearning for milk persists. You can gently sway or stroll with the baby, yet the wailing only amplifies. Each time the pacifier is placed in their mouth, they'll suck on it, but as soon as they recognize no nourishment is flowing, they'll promptly expel it. A hunger for life will manifest in your soul and spirit and nothing will be able to feed it other than truth. It is the hunger to align with God's original plan for your life. You have a hunger to live out your purpose and destiny and nothing will substitute. You will cry out until you get it. *Matthew 5:6 KJV "Blessed are they which do hunger and thirst after righteousness: for they shall be filled."* You've endured numerous individuals extracting from you, failing to provide sufficient or reciprocal contributions. You aspire for a superior existence, one where you can fully embrace life's richness. It has been said that when you're happy you listen to the beat of the song, the music. But when you are in pain, you listen to the words. It is the pain of life that causes us to discern the patterns, seasons, and cycles of our lives.

The setbacks of your past will not hijack your future. Keep digging and you will strike oil. At times it is going to feel like someone is squeezing the very life out of you. Dig through the hurt, disappointment, unfruitful decisions, misconception, suffering, and pain. One of the biggest mistakes a person can make is to give themselves away before they know who they are. Why is this such a detrimental mistake? Because when you do not know your identity, some unauthorized person will attempt to give you one. *Galatians 3:1 NLT - "Oh, foolish Galatians! Who has cast an evil spell on you? For the meaning of Jesus Christ's death was made as clear to you as if you had seen a picture of his death on the cross."*

Diving deeper into my upbringing reveals the intricate formation of patterns. Growing up, my parents taught me many things. However, some things were more prevalently taught than others. My father was a hardworking man who received salvation later in his life, mother was also a hard worker. My father taught me work ethic in a distinct kind of way. My mother also taught me the work ethic and the posture of prayer. Notice I didn't say she taught me how to pray, she taught me the "posture of prayer". I used to think my father was insane. I can remember when I was a little girl, my dad would make me get up on Saturdays around 7 a.m. to make up my bed and clean up. I would say, "Daddy it is Saturday morning; I want to lay in bed and watch cartoons, all my friends in bed too." He would fuss and say, "GET UP!". I would be so angry, but you dare not say anything back to your parents back then. I would get up, make my bed, and sit in the chair. He would then say, "Don't no man want no lazy woman". I would look like what are you talking about? I don't even want a man, I just want to watch cartoons, I was a little girl. My dad would tell me this almost every day – "Don't no man want no lazy woman". During my childhood to young adulthood, I heard these words repeatedly from him. The echoes of his statement lingered within me for countless years. The seeds of those words were sown into my soul.

He would call me outside to help him work on cars, from transmission work, replacing brakes, fixing flats, and changing oil. My father likely aimed to convey the importance of persistent effort, unwavering diligence, and a refusal to concoct excuses in life. His message underscored the need for self-reliance and discouraging reliance on others for support. He emphasized the willingness to take on multiple jobs if the situation demanded, acknowledging that life's path can be riddled with challenges, yet urging against surrender in the face of inconvenience.

Initially, it was brutal getting up on Saturdays around 7 a.m. But as time passed it became easier. I started getting up to make my bed before he told me. He would enter the room and simply observe, seldom expressing pride or giving compliments. Nevertheless, I could discern his contentment from the expression on his face. I recall his hospitalization, during which he lay on his deathbed. I said, "Daddy, do you remember when you would always tell me, 'Don't no man want no lazy woman,' and you made me get up early on Saturday mornings?" He smiled and replied, "Yes, I do." I asked, "Why didn't you make the boys, my brothers, get up too?" He explained, "Because you had a teachable spirit." I nodded and said, "Okay, Daddy," and we both smiled. Then, it occurred to me, and I added, "I'm not sure why this thought never came to mind before, but, Daddy, did you ever consider that 'Don't no woman want a lazy man'?" He burst into laughter. Well, that was my last conversation with my dad, because the next morning he made his transition. My mother also instilled in me a strong work ethic and the practice of prayer. She displayed unwavering dedication by consistently going to work, regardless of the circumstances or her personal feelings. Additionally, she made sure we attended church regularly. One consistent aspect of my mother's life was her nightly prayers. My room was next to hers and I would watch her. She didn't know I was watching her. However, at that time, she never prayed out loud, the only thing she said out loud was Amen. Therefore, I say she taught me the posture of prayer. I began to mimic her, when she got on her knees, I would get on mine, never saying a word, never knowing what to say. I would be on my knees with my eyes closed. When she got up to say Amen, I got up and said Amen. This went on for years. As I got older, I started saying words I learned in church and Sunday school. Prayers like "Now I lay me down to sleep I pray to the Lord my soul to keep, if I should die before I wake, I pray to the Lord my soul to take, Amen". Then I would repeat the *23rd Psalms*. For the record, my mother has transformed into a formidable prayer warrior, fearlessly lifting up prayers, irrespective of location or audience, interceding fervently for anyone and everyone. I want to emphasize that despite the challenges we faced, my parents and siblings always loved me; we are a family bound by love.

Rules became the bedrock upon which the structure of my existence was erected. They acted as guiding principles that not only shaped my actions but also framed my perceptions, influencing the way I navigated through the world around me. I remain uncertain about the events that unfolded in my father's past or his upbringing that led him to consistently voice these sentiments to me: "Don't no man want no lazy woman", because my mother certainly was not lazy. Looking back, it becomes evident that some event or individual had inflicted wounds upon my father, leading to the formation of patterns in his life that were then passed down to me. These deep-seated wounds and the words that emanated from his lips would significantly influence my future for many years. My upbringing lacked balance; it consistently emphasized my obligations. My father taught me to hold high standards for myself, but not how to expect that from others. I was an exceptionally diligent student, consistently achieving honor roll status even when I became pregnant during high school. Dad did not realize that he was grooming me for a perfect storm. This set the tone for future relationships. Remember, this had been embedded in my head and then in my heart, so I was able to adapt to very strenuous situations and relationships. *Proverbs 23:7 KJV - "As a man thinketh in his heart so is he."* I was never a stranger to hard work. It was like a coach telling a player not to lose the ball. I knew how to protect, build, nurture, cover, and provide for. It felt like an animal being marked with a branding iron; the sensation was imprinted on me. No matter what I went through in life, I never stopped working. No matter the pain, rejection, sickness, disappointment, or manipulation, I knew I had to work. As I think back, when I told Dad "Don't no woman want no lazy man," he just laughed, and I laughed too. The full extent of the pain and bewilderment that this would sow in my life remained elusive to me. From my father to boyfriends, and eventually to a husband, I grappled with comprehending authentic, mutual relationships. These connections seemed to hinge on predefined roles rather than genuine connections. The other person always told me what I was supposed to be doing or compared me with someone else, rarely defining their role. I was a Daddy's girl; I loved my dad but it would be years later that I would realize that I had Daddy issues. I had been groomed to work hard and weather storms but rarely received affirmations. I adapted to moving through life without closure and clarity. All these things shifted me to a lack of self-worth and confidence. My older brothers were overprotective. I was aware of their love for me, but they were quite restrictive when it came to dating or engaging in any activities. I recall a specific incident one night when I was planning to attend a party with a friend. I had laid out my clothes on the bed, which consisted of a T-shirt and biking shorts. After taking a shower, I discovered that my biking shorts had mysteriously disappeared. My brother had got them and burned them up. I sat on the bed and cried. In retrospect, something painful was in my brother that led him to burn my clothes. What type of seeds had been planted in him to cause those heinous actions? What was he translating and transferring to me? His actions were controlling my mindset. My thought was, I must be doing something wrong for him to behave like that. So, my solution was to stop wearing biking shorts. I did not have the problem, he had the problem, but I made a choice to conform to his mindset and controlling ways. Let's explore and examine three key influences that have shaped my life thus far: "Don't no man want no lazy woman", the posture of prayer, and the spirit of control.

"Don't no man want no lazy woman" formed the root of imposter syndrome. This instilled within me a mindset of prioritizing others' contentment over my well-being. I possessed a strong belief in my work, yet my self-confidence was lacking. My achievements felt undeserved, and my sense of value seemed to hinge on the approval of others. I was taught the importance of giving but struggled to accept anything in return. I navigated life while neglecting my own needs to enhance the lives of those around me. My upbringing groomed me for roles, but genuine reciprocal relationships were elusive. I developed a tendency to prioritize pleasing others and became a people-pleaser at my core. It took many years before I grasped the concept of grace, a concept that was largely absent from my upbringing dominated by rules. These words I internalized led me to act out of fear rather than love. Fear, as I learned, brings torment, while love empowers. Those same words became the reason I found myself in perfect storms without adequate protection. This perspective left me feeling inadequate and believing that I deserved any hardships I encountered. The absence of personal affirmations from my father sent me on an unsettling journey fraught with doubt.

The posture of prayer formed the root of religion vs relationship. I saw my mom get on her knees to pray to God, which displayed a physical form of reverence to God. I was living life with moral absolutes but not in a meaningful way. It would take several years before I started comprehending the true nature of God, His love, and his original purpose for my life. I came to realize that He was a God with whom I could openly share my deepest thoughts and desires. However, due to my uncertainty about what to say in prayer, my prayers remained quite vague and general during that time; I did not want to offend God. I was always afraid to live life because I wanted to be right in the sight of God and man. This physical form of reverence caused me to go into the perfect storm without the relational advantage of truly knowing God. Hence, I did not understand God's authentic love, power, and grace.

Control became the foundation of shaping and signifying a desire for compliance. Whenever my brother would burn my clothes, I refrained from asking why or confronting him. I somehow believed that I must be doing something inherently wrong, something that displeased him and God. This led me to constantly seek approval in nearly everything I did, resulting in the establishment of personal constraints and a reluctance to express myself. People often attempt to exert control over others as a means to conceal their inner turmoil. Such behavior can also be considered a manifestation of witchcraft and manipulation. Roots of imposter syndrome, religion, and control are ingredients for a perfect storm. These roots are poisonous and detrimental to the soul, body, and spirit.

I found myself pregnant during my teenage years, and it felt like my entire world came to a halt. I had been an active cheerleader and a top-performing student with straight "A"s in high school. I couldn't help but wonder what this meant for my life and future. At the age of 17, I gave birth to my daughter. My dad's teachings about hard work kicked into high gear, and my mom's lessons on prayer became even more crucial. My dedication to prayer deepened as I took on the responsibility of caring for this delicate, precious, and exceptionally lovely little girl. If I knew anything, I knew I would provide for her and cover her in prayer. We're still in the process of uncovering, discovering, and recovering. I distinctly recall a moment before I became pregnant when I was singing in the choir. After our performance, I heard a voice that seemed as though someone was sitting right next to me, speaking directly to me. The voice said, stop having sex, the person you are with is not your husband. I grew up in a very traditional Baptist church, no one talked about hearing God and stuff like that. The choir sang, the preacher preached, we had communion, and sang the last song – "Reach out and touch somebody's hand, make this world a better place if you can you". I was startled at the words I heard but I knew it was God. I told my friend what God had spoken to me, and she said well God didn't tell me that, in other words, I'm going to keep having sex. I wanted someone to walk the journey with me. No matter how you ignore God, His word and warnings will come to pass in your life. God was telling me to stop having sex because He knew the road ahead.

I would become pregnant by a man who was not ordained by God to be a part of my future, God clearly said, he is not your husband. *Romans 8:28 NLT - "And we know that God causes everything to work together] for the good of those who love God and are called according to his purpose for them."* My daughter and children are the best part of me. Someone asked me if I was going to get an abortion, and I said no. I was willing to fight for her no matter what. This same child I fought to provide the best life possible, she would later become a woman and fight for my spiritual liberation!

Uncovering allows you to discern that something is wrong, you must be willing to admit, as I did, that something unauthorized is there. Is there something that you tucked away, ignored, tried to discard, tried to forget, extremely embarrassed about, tried to bandage up? Is there a wound that you wrapped up, never getting it diagnosed, never treating it, never getting healed? Many times, when things are too hurtful or fearful to address or acknowledge, we cover them up. Individuals endure years of immersing themselves in their work or dedicating all their time to their children. These are important, but when you use them as a crutch or a drug to lessen the pain of an issue, it's only a matter of time before the infection of the pain starts to ooze from underneath the bandages. If that thing you covered up is still causing you to hemorrhage out joy, peace, wholeness, or your identity, it's not covered up, you are. You thought you could cover it up and move on, but it has you hostage, it steals your dreams, vision, happiness, motivation, and possibilities. It steals your present and your future.

The assailant is not a person with a gun but it's deception attacking your perception, its fear attacking your power, it is guilt attacking God's grace. All these powerful demonic, deceptive forces are coming against your mind, which in turn, triggers false emotions, feeding you lies, then attempts to destroy your destiny. *2 Corinthians 10:4 KJV - "For the weapons of our warfare are not carnal, but mighty through God to the pulling down of strongholds."* Deception, fear, and guilt are not carnal weapons, they are thought patterns that put you in a cycle. When these habitual patterns of thought enter your mind, it can take years to identify the real culprit. When something can't be defined, it can't be aligned. The battlefield is in your mind. It is not what others think of you that causes you defeat, but what you think of yourself.

Exploring the fascinating realm of psychology, let's delve deeper into the intricate phenomenon known as Stockholm Syndrome. Stockholm Syndrome is said to be a coping mechanism for a captive or abusive situation. It is stated that many medical professionals consider the victim's positive feelings toward their abuser a psychological response, a coping mechanism that they use to survive. What makes this phenomenon even more surprising is the extent to which victims may go in defending their abusers even after being liberated from their tormentors. This loyalty to their captors can persist long after the physical captivity has ended, often leaving outsiders baffled by their continued attachment to the abuse and dysfunction they've endured. Stockholm Syndrome stands as a stark reminder of the intricate interplay between the human mind and extreme adversity, shedding light on the striking, and at times baffling, ways in which individuals adapt to traumatic situations in their quest for survival.

God is beckoning you to reveal the moment and location where you hid the thing that hurt you. In essence, you took it upon yourself to conclude that this situation was beyond God's ability to address, and so you buried it deep within, all the while continuing to bear the scars. In *John 11*, there were two sisters, Mary, and Martha whose brother died, his name was Lazarus. The scripture says Jesus loved Lazarus. When Jesus got there, Lazarus had been in the grave for four days. The sisters were angry with Jesus, they said if you had been here our brother would have not died. Jesus said show me where you laid him. They said he's been in the grave for four days, he stinks now, his body is corroded, and there is no use now. There is nothing you or anyone can do. His reply was show me where you laid him. He told them I am the one who raises the dead and gives life. *John 11:41-44 NLT "So they rolled the stone aside. Then Jesus looked up to heaven and said, "Father, thank you for hearing me. You always hear me, but I said it out loud for the sake of all these people standing here, so that they will believe you sent me." Then Jesus shouted, "Lazarus, come out!" And the dead man came out, his hands and feet bound in graveclothes, his face wrapped in a headcloth. Jesus told them, "Unwrap him and let him go!"*

I desire for you to know and receive the truth that God has declared your resurrection, liberty, and victory! He has decreed every dead thing to lose you and let you go! Take off those grave clothes, God is giving you according to *Isaiah 61:3 KJV "Beauty for ashes, the oil of joy for mourning, the garment of praise for the spirit of heaviness; that they might be called trees of righteousness, the planting of the Lord, that he might be glorified."* God has awakened you to a life the devil tried to steal from you. As you have embarked on this quest for revelation, you are on the brink of uncovering the magnificent design that God has laid out for your life—a design filled with goodness. It's time to leave behind the falsehoods, not just your own, but those of others, as well as the weight of sickness, the sickness of others, the shadows of fear, the fears imposed by others, the veil of erroneous doctrine, the darkness of depression, the weight of grief, and the fragments of brokenness, all of which resemble the chains that once confined you within that metaphorical grave. Lock them away and cast aside the key. Be grateful that you have awakened, vowing never again to neglect the identity bestowed upon you by God. You are awake!

Chapter 2 – The Trauma of Waking Up

I'm convinced that we Black women possess a special inde-structible strength that allows us to not only get down, but to get up, to get through, and to get over. - Janet Jackson

After emerging from a traumatic experience, medical professionals often conduct thorough examinations to assess the extent of physical injuries. During these evaluations, they employ tactile methods, asking patients if they can perceive sensations in specific areas. However, trauma extends beyond the physical realm; it can profoundly affect one's emotional and psychological well-being. In some cases, the traumatic events, interpersonal challenges, and toxic relationships one has endured can leave lasting emotional scars that form akin to a form of emotional paralysis. Surviving the trauma is undoubtedly a remarkable feat, similar to awakening from a prolonged emotional coma. Yet, amidst the journey to recovery, something vital may have been lost—the ability to connect with one's own emotions and sense of direction. This emotional aftermath can leave individuals feeling adrift, and unsure of their emotional mobility and the path ahead. While physical wounds may heal, the intangible wounds of trauma may persist, leaving survivors grappling with a profound sense of disconnection from themselves and the world around them. In the wake of such experiences, it becomes crucial to embark on a healing journey that not only mends the visible wounds but also helps regain a sense of emotional mobility and purpose.

Similarly, with medical procedures or surgeries, upon waking, you often experience discomfort. Depending on the severity of the condition, this discomfort can escalate into trauma, particularly as the effects of anesthesia gradually subside. Initially, there was pain because of the sickness or disease being present, but now the pain is from the sickness or disease being removed. The reassuring aspect of this situation is that the pain, illness, and hardship have reached their expiration date. By this time, you may have endured considerable suffering, but you are now on the path toward recovery, or perhaps it would be more fitting to call it a process of restoration. This phase is critical, and it's important to proceed with caution, attentiveness, and vigilance. It's during this period that some individuals can become ensnared, allowing the pain of their past to rob them of a potentially extraordinary future. This strategy aligns with the adversary's intentions. The enemy schemes to wear you down to the point where, even when God offers deliverance, you find yourself too exhausted, financially strained, mentally fatigued, and spiritually depleted to embrace the blessings that await you. You will be at the door but too fatigued or fearful to cross the threshold. It is the phase where you make it out of the wilderness but are too tired and broken to walk in the promised land. You can see the blessing but ponder if you have enough strength to embrace it. Know that God has remembered you just like he did Hagar in *Genesis 16:13 "The God Who Sees Me," translated as "El Roi"* in Hebrew. However, just as God remembered her, some despised her. As you are healing, you will attempt to fight others who are coming against you. You need to muster the courage to let God take charge of your battles. Remember, you've undergone a significant operation, and it's vital to prioritize complete healing. This is a time to rest, surround yourself with genuine, loving individuals, and ready yourself for the forthcoming blessings. I could have concluded the story at your awakening, but there's a wealth of experiences yet to unfold, and you must be present to witness them. Some individuals wake up and break free from malevolent, unproductive, or controlling circumstances, only to return to the same patterns. It's known as recurring cycles. Seasons change with time; cycles change with people. It's a beautiful thing to wake up but there's still more work to do and some of it will be hard and challenging but you can do it. When you are discharged from the hospital after having a procedure, you receive care and follow-up instructions. You have awoken, but the individuals surrounding you remain spiritually disconnected. Some of these people have bene-fited from your previous illness, brokenness, and dysfunction, and they may still attempt to exert control over you during your recovery phase. They might utter phrases like, "What happened to you? We just want things to return to the way they were," essentially urging you to revert to your previous state or re-enter a cycle of dysfunction. They aim to perpetuate the destruction of your life, defile your well-being, maintain their control over you, manipulate you, deceive you, threaten you, project their fears and issues onto you, and accompany them on a purposeless journey to nowhere. They persist in making requests without undergoing personal change, often appending scripture to their demands. God has blessed you with the profound strength and unwavering courage to once again embrace your deepest desires. You desire healing, ful-fillment, fairness, respect, freedom, God's promises operating in your life, joy, peace, happiness, adventure, true companionship, and love. You want your Kairos Moment and you deserve it! Your eyes are open and you are seeing clearer. Upon awakening, indi-viduals who lack fulfillment and self-contentment attempt to pro-ject their discontent onto you, aiming to make you feel unworthy. Without exercising caution, you could inadvertently transform into your adversary. Guilt, frustration, anger, and confusion will at-tempt to overtake you. You can find yourself caught between the life you have and the life God is offering you. However, it's im-portant to understand that even though God has opened your eyes, you still must be led by the Holy Spirit and keep a pure heart. God will guide you every step of the journey. When the children of Israel cried out from Egypt because of their bondage, God remembered His covenant with Abraham, Issac, and Jacob, and delivered them. *Exodus 2:23-25 "23 After a long time, the king of Egypt died. The Israelites groaned and cried out under their burden of slavery, and their cry for deliverance from bondage ascended to God. 24 So God heard their groaning, and He remembered His covenant with Abraham, Isaac, and Jacob. 25 God saw the Israelites and took notice."*

The children of Israel woke up from slavery and cried to be free. God knew exactly how to deal with Pharoah. You must seek God in your exodus, doing it on your own can cause movements out-of-season and collateral damage. Listen intently for God's exit strategy. This process is crucial and will prevent you from reverting to your past mistakes. *Proverbs 26:11 "As a dog returns to its vomit, so fools repeat their folly."* Bear in mind, some individuals around you, benefitted and profited from your dysfunction and sickness. They will not rejoice in your awakening and might endeavor to shatter you, aiming to bring misery to your life in an attempt to regain control. During your exit, your opponent will endeavor to create obstacles, subjecting you to immense suffering through affliction and deceit, as outlined in verse 9.

Exodus 5:1-9 NIV 1 Afterward Moses and Aaron went to Pharaoh and said, "This is what the Lord, the God of Israel, says: 'Let my people go, so that they may hold a festival to me in the wilderness." 2 Pharaoh said, "Who is the Lord, that I should obey him and let Israel go? I do not know the Lord and I will not let Israel go." 3 Then they said, "The God of the Hebrews has met with us. Now let us take a three-day journey into the wilderness to offer sacrifices to the Lord our God, or he may strike us with plagues or with the sword." 4 But the king of Egypt said, "Moses and Aaron, why are you taking the people away from their labor? Get back to your work!" 5 Then Pharaoh said, "Look, the people of the land are now numerous, and you are stopping them from working." 6 That same day Pharaoh gave this order to the slave drivers and overseers in charge of the people: 7 "You are no longer to supply the people with straw for making bricks; let them go and gather their own straw. 8 But require them to make the same number of bricks as before; don't reduce the quota. They are lazy; that is why they are crying out, 'Let us go and sacrifice to our God.' 9 Make the work harder for the people so that they keep working and pay no attention to lies."

Should you encounter a Pharaoh-like presence in your life, be aware that this spirit embodies selfishness, ruthlessness, manipulation, and fear. It recognizes that it's losing its grip on you, and if you successfully break free, others will witness your triumph and be inspired to do the same. Always remember that when you emerge victorious, you pave the way for others to follow suit. Observing you will provide them with the inspiration they need to foster self-belief. You are removing the false king from the throne of your mind and exposing it at the same time. You have been touched, healed, and delivered by the almighty God but your enemy does not like it. That spirit monopolized you from your inability to think clearly. It will try to turn your resurrection into a crucifixion by trying to crucify you, trap you, set you up, and defame your character. They know you have become a threat to their demonic schemes and kingdoms of darkness. They will try employing the same malevolent strategies to return you to a state of unconsciousness. You must arm yourself with the armor of God. *Ephesians 6:10-18 10 Finally, be strong in the Lord and in his mighty power. 11 Put on the full armor of God, so that you can take your stand against the devil's schemes. 12 For our struggle is not against flesh and blood, but against the rulers, against the authorities, against the powers of this dark world and against the spiritual forces of evil in the heavenly realms. 13 Therefore put on the full armor of God, so that when the day of evil comes, you may be able to stand your ground, and after you have done everything, to stand. 14 Stand firm then, with the belt of truth buckled around your waist, with the breastplate of righteousness in place, 15 and with your feet fitted with the readiness that comes from the gospel of peace. 16 In addition to all this, take up the shield of faith, with which you can extinguish all the flaming arrows of the evil one. 17 Take the helmet of salvation and the sword of the Spirit, which is the word of God. 18 And pray in the Spirit on all occasions with all kinds of prayers and requests. With this in mind, be alert and always keep on praying for all the Lord's people.*

You are about to embark on a journey of uncovering or reacquainting yourself with the kingdom mandate, a profound directive that encompasses not only purpose but also the bestowed authority. This path will grant you a distinct perspective; your vision will be reframed, your hearing will be attuned to a new frequency, and your perception will be filtered through a transformed mindset. *Ephesians 1:18 KJV - "The eyes of your understanding being enlightened; that ye may know what is the hope of his calling, and what the riches of the glory of his inheritance in the saints".* Asking questions will be a part of the awakening process because you're identifying and addressing seeds that were planted in you while you were asleep or should I say dysfunctional. *Matthew 13:25 NLT - "But that night as the workers slept, his enemy came and planted weeds among the wheat, then slipped away."* You embark on a journey of reflection, meticulously revisiting conversations, navigating through various situations, dissecting seasons, and deciphering recurring cycles and decisions, all in your pursuit of clarity. This expedition may occasionally stir emotions of anger and frustration, which initially find expression outwardly before turning inward. You find yourself grappling with self-doubt, pondering the rationale behind past choices, and even exclaiming, "What on earth was I thinking?" This phase of the process holds the potential to become a stumbling block if not handled with care. It's essential to remember that your previous state of being was linked to a toxic situation and other attributes that were not ordained by God. However, your current trajectory is leading you towards a position of empowerment within the kingdom, driven by the revelations you have received.

During your time in bondage, you developed the skill of adjusting to a life that fell short of your God-given potential. You became accustomed to serving under the dominion of bondage, doubt, pain, depression, dysfunction, and disbelief. Now, you must acquire the aptitude to thrive in a state of kingship, happiness, mental clarity, joy, peace, and prosperity. In this process, you are uncovering your inherent self-worth. Even if your eyes have been opened, and your body has been restored to health, a process of mental transformation remains necessary. *Romans 12:2 NLT - "Don't copy the behavior and customs of this world, but let God transform you into a new person by changing the way you think. Then you will learn to know God's will for you, which is good and pleasing and perfect."*

Consider an individual emerging from a coma—inevitably, they'll grapple with agitation and confusion. It's natural to be laden with questions. Thoughts about life's trajectory and the seeming detachment from it for so long become prominent. Contemplations on age arise, realizing that a substantial portion of envisioned goals remains unfulfilled. A sense of being trapped and unwell sets in. Amidst this introspection, a crucial juncture emerges—you must confront the reflection in the mirror—the reflection of yourself. Look at yourself and give yourself GRACE, you survived what was intended to kill you. It is important to build yourself up and forgive yourself if needed. You are accepting accountability for yourself from this point forward. People can only control, misman-age, manipulate, and deceive you if you allow them to. It is imper-ative to cultivate your relationship with God, you need wisdom and understanding. *Proverbs 4:7 KJV - "Wisdom is the principal thing; therefore, get wisdom: and with all thy getting get understanding."* You cannot be successful at something that you don't understand and to be successful in this life, you will need the wisdom of God. Anything that cannot be defined, cannot be aligned.

Confession:

Father, I thank you that I have AWAKENED! I decree and declare that I am a testament to your goodness and mercy. You have awak-ened me to new possibilities. You have healed my body and my mind. You have caused me to smile again. You have delivered me from the snares of my enemies. You have shielded me from false accusations, you have turned my sorrow into joy, you have favored me according to Isaiah 61 by giving me a crown of beauty instead of ashes, the oil of joy, instead of mourning, and a garment of praise, instead of a spirit of despair. I will forever partner with you to live out my God-given identity. I will not operate in fear, I wel-come new opportunities, adventures, and relationships. I decree that I am blessed coming and going. I thank you, God, that peace, prosperity, and protection shall be my portion. You have restored unto me the joy of my salvation. I am healed and made whole in the name of Jesus.

The key element that propelled my thriving after awakening was my unwavering commitment to self-reflection. I diligently adhered to the prescribed care instructions and immersed myself in the teachings of the Word of God, ensuring daily application. Staying closely connected with my small circle of friends and family was pivotal. They played a crucial role in preserving the zest for life within me. Their constant reminders held me accountable for my well-being and self-worth. They encouraged me to embrace every aspect of my femininity and freedom. Persistently gazing at my reflection in the mirror became a symbolic practice, a constant reminder of what I had endured and how far I had come. I solemnly pledged to never forget or forsake myself again. This was a transformative journey, reshaping both my inner being and my outward appearance. Each day, I renewed my commitment never to neglect or lose sight of my true self.

James 1:22-25 NLT 22 But don't just listen to God's word. You must do what it says. Otherwise, you are only fooling yourselves. 23 For if you listen to the word and don't obey, it is like glancing at your face in a mirror. 24 You see yourself, walk away, and forget what you look like. 25 But if you look carefully into the perfect law that sets you free, and if you do what it says and don't forget what you heard, then God will bless you for doing it.

Engaging in work became my way of managing the challenges I faced. Research shows unhealthy coping strategies encompass a broad spectrum, including excessive work, substance abuse, alcohol misuse, pornography, indulging in excess, isolating oneself, intrusive thoughts, and more. For me, immersing myself in work acted as a numbing agent, blinding me to the underlying issues. It was like being in a spiritual coma, a state that permitted me to embrace the pain and dysfunction. Anything you choose to disregard becomes something you will not confront. I was engaged in self-deception, essentially postponing the inevitable change. My life needed a transformation. While there were gains on one front, there were losses on another. I was gaining financial wealth but neglecting the joy, peace, fulfillment, and happiness of life. In certain aspects, I was prioritizing work above my relationship with God. Embracing the life that God had planned for me required facing myself in the mirror and committing to the effort needed for meaningful change. This dedicated effort helped me cultivate self-love, self-appreciation, and recognition of my value. As a result, I began to rekindle my dreams and envision the beautiful life that God had in store for me.

The trust and assurance I acquired in God propelled me to speak His word and anticipate transformation. My life was undergoing a remarkable shift right before my eyes. I began to employ God's principles to disrupt and dismantle the worldly and demonic systems at play. I exercised caution in my speech, avoiding negative declarations. I steered clear of hostile environments, cultivating a regular and impassioned prayer life, frequently fasting, and consistently delving into the Word of God. I sowed financial seeds, constructed a vision board, partnered with individuals aligned with the kingdom's values, provided encouragement, and offered prayers for others. Additionally, I temporarily scaled back my work commitments. God was calling me higher, and I had to dedicate more time to Him to be equipped for the journey. God was preparing me for something so much bigger than me. Just as God was preparing me for something bigger, He is also preparing you for something bigger. I say unto you as Jesus said to the Jairus daughter, who they declared was dead, Jesus took her by the hand and said unto her *Talitha cumi*, which means damsel arise. I prophesy to you that you will arise, you will not die here, God is waking you up, getting you up, getting you ready and you will live again, you will fulfill your purpose; it is time for your destiny to manifest. I say to you get up and take your rightful place in the Kingdom of God! You are a miracle, let God astonish the world with your awakening!

Mark 5:41 KJV - And he took the damsel by the hand, and said unto her, Talitha cumi, which is, being interpreted, Damsel, I say unto thee arise.

Chapter 3 – A Season of Hemorrhaging

I can remember the years of bleeding out. I was hemorrhaging out joy, peace, love, health, happiness, sanity, finances, fulfillment, my God-given identity, and sacred desires. As a Pastor, I ministered to many people when I was broken and was wounded myself. In roles spanning from wife and mother to Pastor and friend, I poured out my heart selflessly, even during moments when I craved care and solace for myself more than anything else. I was not sharing from my overflow; I was sharing from my last reserves until, over time, my wellspring ran dry. I had poured myself out completely, leaving nothing behind. Imagine using a straw to chase every last drop around the rim of a cup, even then, not a trace remained. It felt like I had emptied every ounce of my being. My sense of disillusionment was profound, my strength waned, confusion reigned, hopelessness set in, and I shattered into pieces. My life was in a deadly spiral; I was sick in body, spirit, and soul.

Enduring a serious condition while continually receiving incorrect diagnoses is an incredibly distressing and profoundly unsettling experience. The frustration and uncertainty that accompany such a situation can take an immense toll on both one's physical well-being and emotional state, leading to a sense of helplessness and anxiety that permeates every aspect of life. Several years back, I found myself in the clutches of a debilitating illness. Its relentless progression brought me to the brink of despair. I became a frequent visitor to the doctor's office, tormented by excruciating abdominal and back pain that seemed unending. At certain moments, simply walking became an agonizing struggle. The pain was of such unbearable magnitude that it would violently rouse me from my sleep. I was continually misdiagnosed and was given prescriptions that did not heal. After a day of working, I decided to walk around the block to get some fresh air. I barely made it back to the building. The pain had become unbearable and I was short of breath. I found myself unable to drive, relying on one of my employees to escort me to an Urgent Care facility. It was within those walls that I finally received an authentic diagnosis, emotions running high as the truth came to light. I'll always remember that moment when the doctor examined me while I was doubled over in pain. After a blood test, she advised me I needed to get to the emergency room, expressing concern that my appendix had ruptured. An ambulance hurried me to the hospital where further tests confirmed the diagnosis, and it was determined that emergency surgery was necessary that very night. A surge of emotions swept over me, I was afraid and relieved at the same time. I was so thankful that someone finally identified the origin of the pain. I breathed a sigh of relief because I knew this pain was coming to an end. The pain, sickness and not knowing had reached an expiration date. I was prepped and rolled away for surgery. Once the surgery was complete, the following day, the surgeon took a moment to share her insights. She revealed that, in her experience, my case stood as the most severe she had encountered. The complexity of the situation was such that the surgery had taken twice as long as initially anticipated. Her words bore a weighty emotion as she continued, revealing, "I exerted my utmost to address the situation, but it's possible that you could find yourself back in the hospital due to unforeseen complications." I expressed, "The God that I serve is a source of healing, and what humans consider impossible is achievable through divine power." In response, she glanced at me and responded with an acknowledgment, saying, "Alright." During the surgery, a tube was inserted into my stomach to assist with drainage. Curious about its eventual removal, I longed for reassurance, would I be sedated during the process? The answer I received was far from comforting: "No, we will extract it while you are awake." A mixture of anxiety and anguish tightened its grip as I probed further, "Will it hurt?" The doctor's frank reply resonated with unfiltered truth, acknowledging that the experience would give rise to profound discomfort.

Deep within, I recognized that 'uncomfortable' was an understatement, it was destined to inflict searing pain. On the day of my discharge, two nurses came in to remove the tube. We engaged in a back-and-forth exchange during the process. My anxiety made me vocalize my fear, repeatedly requesting a halt. I urged for honesty, emphasizing the impending agony, to which she acknowledged, "Yes, ma'am, it will be painful, but the discomfort will be brief." One of the nurses offered support by holding my hand, while the other nurse executed the removal on the count of three. The sensation was excruciating, as though my very insides were being torn apart. However, one undeniable truth emerged from the experience: the pain of the tube's removal was indeed short-lived. Removing poisonous and toxic things, people, and situations out of your life may be painful but the pain won't last long. The tube had to be removed because it was no longer needed, the surgery was over, and the drainage ceased. It was time to start the recovery process. Trying to recover elements or connections that no longer matter is a pointless effort that hinders progress and wastes time.

As time progressed, spanning days and weeks, my overall well-being improved, yet a lingering issue persisted. I continued to experience shortness of breath, prompting my return to the emergency room. Subsequent examinations and tests revealed the presence of lung nodules, likely stemming from the prior infection. They referred me to a specialist, in which they said they would like to put me under observation for a while. On my first visit, the specialist confirmed what the ER had advised. I was heartbroken. I cried and then sat in silence. By the second year, they said you have more spots on your lungs, but they do not appear to be cancerous. I underwent significant emotional and physical turmoil, due to my inability to walk long distances, I was granted a temporary handicap parking tag, intensifying my sense of vulnerability and frustration. Vividly etched in my memory is the experience of reaching the third-year milestone. During that time, I occupied the waiting area, anticipating my turn to be summoned for the X-ray procedure. I said these few words: "God, I'm tired, I can't go on like this. You are my healer; I trust you with every part of my body. If it pleases you, please heal my body, in the name of Jesus". After I said the prayer, they called my name, and an x-ray examination was performed. Nevertheless, on this occasion, the atmosphere was distinctly unusual as they all appeared perplexed. The doctor inquired, "Would you be willing to undergo another X-ray? There seems to be an anomaly, and we must confirm the accuracy of what we're observing." I consented with a simple "alright." Afterwards we sat down together for him to give me the results as usual. He said Mrs. Wilson, we don't see a spot anywhere on your lungs. He was amazed. He said this must be a divine intervention. I said it certainly is. God has healed me, and I will forever give Him praise! He said you no longer have to be seen in this clinic again, and no follow-up is needed. I exited the clinic crying, giving God praise, and praying for others as I was leaving. I wish to emphasize that the extent of your suffering and the duration of your pain are temporary. God has the power and willingness to bring healing.

From that point onwards, this matter has never troubled me. Such is the outcome when God heals you and restores your completeness. God gave me a second chance at life. The surgeon told me that I was a walking miracle and that if that infection had stayed in my body longer, I probably would not be here today.

Let's look at this from another aspect, there was a woman with an issue of blood for twelve long years in *Luke 8:43-48 NLT - "43 And a woman having an issue of blood twelve years, which had spent all her living upon physicians, neither could be healed of any, 44 Came behind him, and touched the border of his garment: and immediately her issue of blood stanched. 45 And Jesus said, Who touched me? When all denied, Peter and they that were with him said, Master, the multitude throng thee and press thee, and sayest thou, Who touched me? 46 And Jesus said Somebody hath touched me: for I perceive that virtue is gone out of me. 47 And when the woman saw that she was not hid, she came trembling, and falling down before him, she declared unto him before all the people for what cause she had touched him, and how she was healed immediately. 48 And he said unto her, Daughter, be of good comfort: thy faith hath made thee whole; go in peace."*

This woman experienced a hemorrhage, which involved severe bleeding. Not only was she physically losing blood, but she was also financially drained due to unsuccessful medical treatments, burdened by the constant foul odor from her condition, and emotionally isolated because she was deemed unclean. Neverthe-

less, she summoned the strength of her faith and made a coura-
geous decision to emerge from her seclusion, exposing herself to
the crowd to reach Jesus. She stepped out of hiding. The pain and
trauma of waking up will cause you to come out of hiding and go
through a forceful multitude of people pressing up against each
other. She had enough faith to believe that Jesus could do what no
other power could, and she knew it was her time. She prevailed
over fear and pressed her way to touch Jesus so much so that she
drew virtue out of him.

A crucial aspect to highlight is that people frequently conceal
their suffering, and when God brings about healing, they may attempt to remain hidden. Nevertheless, in this instance, God specifi-
cally called her out. He inquired, "Who touched me?" She could
not remain concealed and approached Him, trembling with awe
and vulnerability. Her miracle was bigger than her embarrassment
or fear. It was vital that she felt no shame and that her experience
was not hidden away. Essentially, this was a deliberate arrange-
ment. After she openly disclosed her entire journey and her mirac-
ulous healing from touching Jesus, He proceeded to make declarations over her. God will not have you made ashamed. In verse 48
he told her to be of good comfort, in other words, do not allow anyone to disrupt your peace and joy from what you receive today.
He also said your faith has made you whole. Whole means, nothing missing, lacking, or broken. She was healed and made whole.
Healing brings deliverance and wholeness brings restoration and
restitution. This means the bleeding stopped, and she received

companionship for all the time she spent alone crying, she received financial blessings and the peace to enjoy it all. As God heals and makes you whole, give Him all the praise, glory, and honor. We've been elaborating on three pillars: uncover, discover, recover. This chapter is all about discovery. Discovery is a game changer. You realize that there is an "After This". *Mark 11:23 You shall have whatever you saith.*

Let's approach this scenario through a lens of spirituality and reality. Allowing the venomous falsehoods of poisonous lies and demonic systems to persist due to ongoing misdiagnoses may jeopardize your very life. Reflect on the duration for which you've been affected by that circumstance, incident, individual, or ailment. Our culture often tends to ignore and suppress issues, adopting a "hush-hush" approach. Similarly, this pattern can be observed in certain religious congregations as well. They emphasize maintaining appearances, even if you're internally shattered. This causes you to feel helpless and hopeless. There's an overwhelming fear that if you find the courage to speak up, they'll unjustly lay blame on you, leaving you devoid of your voice and utterly powerless. It's akin to the experience of a woman who survived rape or a child who has suffered molestation but remains silent. The agony, anguish, and profound psychological and emotional toll permeate every aspect of life, undermining relationships and thwarting any positive opportunities that arise. The toxic burden must be purged. You may have survived it, but you never overcame it. You still wear the clothing of a victim, still broken and battered. An important point to bear is that when you are in survival mode, you do not have time to heal or feel. You are holding on for dear life. God is saying not only do I want to heal you, but I want to make you whole. Like the woman with the issue of blood, God healed her from bleeding out and made her whole through restoration.

Our cultural framework navigates life under the weight of deep-seated fears and the haunting specter of a slave-minded generation. The time has come to unearth the erroneous judgments that have been imposed upon you and to secure a thorough cleansing and healing from the toxic fabrications, deceitful narratives, and at times, wounds that you inflicted upon yourself. Soon, you will realize that you have been molded by a corrosive environment. Similar to the way we seek second opinions in the medical realm, it's now the moment for you to seek guidance from God and listen to the truth. Nevertheless, take comfort in the knowledge that your pleas have reached the divine ear; God's solace is not just a promise but a guarantee of deliverance. Though the path has been paved by God, you must still tread upon it. The days of enduring silent suffering are over.

One day, a dream seized me, a vivid vision of agony and desperation. In the company of my then-husband and a gathering of others, a nightmarish incident unfolded, and a searing gunshot tore through my stomach. My heart sank as I realized I was standing so close to my then-husband and others, yet all seemed utterly unaware of my plight. My body gave way, collapsing to the ground. Amidst the surrounding crowd, not a single soul cast a glance of concern my way, leaving me to grapple with my pain in isolating silence. I took my coat and covered the wound shot. As the blood poured out, I became weaker. It was as though I was ashamed that someone had shot me and felt I needed to hide it. After a while, I opened my coat to look at the wound, and I was bleeding profusely. I said I must get some help, otherwise, I'm not going to make it. Oftentimes, when we are hurt, instead of seeking help, we hide. We become ashamed that various things happened to us. We hide because we know we are weakened but we still must face predators, so we go into seclusion. Concealment often becomes a refuge for those trapped in the clutches of narcissistic individuals, who relentlessly shift blame onto them and perpetually subject them to unfounded accusations.

Considering the dream and the profound challenges I had faced on physical, mental, and spiritual levels, I understood that without assistance, my life was in jeopardy. To seek the help I desperately needed, I had to open up about the struggles I was facing. As the surgeon made an incision into my abdomen to undertake the appendectomy, I found myself sedated and unconscious. There was no sedation for the vulnerability, pain, or embarrassment of what I had been going through. Please hear me when I say that YOU NEED HELP! There are some things you cannot and should not go through alone. If you are with people who refuse to acknowledge your value, you are with the wrong people. I almost had a nervous breakdown suffering in silence. I almost pulled my plug. As I embarked on the journey of counseling and opened up to a select few, the burden began to feel somewhat lighter, offering a glimmer of relief. Nevertheless, I had grown accustomed to dysfunction, and, surprisingly, it posed a significant challenge for me to accept that the circumstances I found myself in were not in alignment with God's will.

Similarly, when an animal is wounded and a person reaches out to help, the animal will strike, putting both lives in danger. Depending on the severity of the wound, humans do the same thing. The injured perceive help as a threat looking to capitalize on their weakened state. It took several years before I opened up to receive help. I felt like those trying to help me were going to hurt me for their motives. So, I would constantly withdraw myself, go into seclusion, and reject the help. Oftentimes, my daughter would text me, sending uplifting messages, and sometimes I would not reply to them. In moments, those texts had the power to stir up a storm of emotions within me. Her words, praising my beauty, hailing me as a queen worthy of happiness. At times, it felt like too much electricity flowing, causing the breaker to trip and the lights to go out. To see what she could see would cost me too much. I was existing and she was encouraging me to live and to recognize my beauty and value. That would necessitate an action I believed I could not accomplish. I felt that was her life and God did not call me to live and be free, I had too many responsibilities and roles to play. I did not have time to dream of freedom or destiny. I was too busy working, taking care of others, making other people's dreams come alive, and being the best mother and wife I could be, but never believed that God had prepared a place and life for me. I saw encouragement, hope, and well wishes to me, at times, as a treat calling me off my post. It would be years later that I would understand that I was also a threat to myself. I built walls so no one could get in but those same walls kept me from getting out. It took years for me to believe that my daughter loved me. When a person has gone through emotional abuse, rejection, mismanagement, control, and other vices, trust does not come easy. Just as the poisonous infection was wrapped all around my intestines and throughout my abdomen, it weakened and affected my entire body. Some of you may be on a deadly collision course because you are hiding, suffering in silence, and continuously getting misdiagnosed. Perhaps you have become a threat or danger to yourself. It is time to present all your hurt, pain, wrong decisions, embarrassment, and suffering to God. He is Jehovah Rapha, the Lord your Healer! We understand that we are all a product of something and some of those seeds that were planted in us connect back to adversities and oppression sent to destroy us before we realize who we are. *We are the righteousness of God by faith in Christ Jesus, Romans 3:22.* God's healing process involved cleansing me of both physical and spiritual toxins and infections. It was like removing the drainage tubes because the issues of leakage and hemorrhaging were finally resolved. God delivered me from unfruitful seeds, seasons, and cycles. Accepting lies that pretend to offer comfort and protection will spread harmful problems in every aspect of your life, aiming to harm, confuse, and break you. Nevertheless, you're embraced by a God whose affection for you is too profound to permit such an ending. This journey might be agonizing, yet I emerged awakened, and so shall you.

Chapter 4 – Passing the Torch

I believe that each of us carries a bit of inner brightness, something unique and individual, a flame that's worth protecting. When we can recognize our light, we become empowered to use it.
- Michelle Obama

We are all influencers in one way or another. In some cases, we pass on things to others unknowingly through our day-to-day living and manner of conversation. "Passing the Torch" is a metaphoric expression that alludes to the ancient Greek torch race, in which a lighted torch was passed from one runner to the next. The light on the torch is very significant. It symbolizes the light of spirit, knowledge, and life. By passing the flame from one person to another in stages, the Torch Relay expresses the handing down of this symbolic fire from generation to generation.

Examining my life, family, and surroundings, I pondered my

essence, and began to examine the "light" on the torch passed to me. Was the light authentic or counterfeit? I shifted my attention to the present and I contemplated the impact I wanted to leave behind, and I reflected on my actions and choices. How true was I to my God-given life? What kind of torch or knowledge was I passing to others? Frequently, an individual's radiance is erroneously attributed to their looks, charm, wealth, and similar attributes. However, these are not the true sources of that radiance. Your light is that beam, image, and likeness given to you by the most high God, the creator of all. *Genesis 1:26-27 "26 Then God said, "Let Us make man in Our image, after Our likeness, to rule over the fish of the sea and the birds of the air, over the livestock, and over all the earth itself and every creature that crawls upon it." 27 So God created man in His own image; in the image of God He created him; male and female He created them."* The light you have is not based or formulated on any external factors. It is a never-dimming light, a torch that shines significantly brighter when you come to the knowledge of who gave it to you and the purpose. This light has dominion, creativity, love, access, and ownership that requires stewardship and management.

I discovered a collection of knowledge that had been transmitted to me over time. However, as I delved deeper into its contents, I discovered the presence of dark elements intertwined within it. This collection encompassed a wide range of emotions and themes, including fear, sorrow, and manipulation. As God awakened me to the knowledge of God in Christ Jesus, I gained enough strength to confront this counterfeit torch. God opened my eyes to a profound understanding as it speaks of in *Ephesians 1:18: pray that your hearts will be flooded with light so that you can understand the confident hope he has given to those he called—his holy people who are his rich and glorious inheritance.* It was as if a light had been switched on within me, empowering me with newfound strength and knowledge. Armed with this spiritual awakening, I found the courage to confront the deceptive nature of this corrupt knowledge that had been embedded in me, realizing that it was nothing but a counterfeit flame, pretending to guide me when, in reality, it led me astray. The light I now hold within me does not just embrace the spiritual realm but also extends to the realm of the natural. Authentic light can unveil all truths. Its intensity was so immense that it unveiled my genuine self, laying bare my identity. Light possesses the incredible ability to rouse every aspect of existence! Light possesses the extraordinary power to stir every facet of existence into awakening! Having undergone a profound awakening and deliverance, it has become my solemn duty to safeguard, nurture, and foster this illumination. Moreover, I am driven to ensure that others are shielded from stumbling into the same pitfalls that once ensnared me.

God wants you to know that He hears your faintest cry. During a revival service at church, I observed people clapping and praising God. It was then that God unveiled a hidden truth to me: beneath their outward appearances of happiness, many were silently struggling and suffocating. Sadly, in some church settings, healing is often postponed or denied due to the actions required for it to manifest. Yet, I share with you the words that God imparted to me during that service: "I hear their faintest cry; I will not let the choir's singing or the preacher's loud sermons drown them out. Let them know that their Redeemer lives and is ready to rescue them. Make it known that I've heard their most subtle pleas. Understand that I have commissioned you to guide them into a deeper understanding through this book. Know that I am a discerning presence amidst the noise in the church. The clamor or tradition within the church cannot drown out the cries of the soul."

The radiance of a bright shining light does not indicate that the light is authentic. Deception does not always appear as it is. Deception can even come through people carrying titles in the church. Satan understands that he is limited in his destruction, so oftentimes, Satan joins an environment that you deem safe, the church, Christian schools, and other religious organizations. This is why the bible speaks of false prophets. God is saying that people will come in His name that he never sent, especially living in the last days as we are in. I am not disregarding the fivefold fellowship ministry as it speaks of in *Ephesians 4:11*. However, had I remained ensnared in the suffocating grip of others' fears, tangled in the web of deceit and manipulation, and failed to grasp the divine purpose mapped out for my existence, I would have become a casualty of deception. I often fell prey to things spoken over my life that were a completely false narrative of the original plan God had for me. Relying on others to feed you spiritually without delving into the depths of God's Word for yourself will lead you to a colossal state of confusion, deception, and error. When you avail yourself to God, He will speak to you. At times, the place of disappointment felt more like home than having a testimony of restoration, restitution, and vindication. There was a widow in the bible who settled in her mind that she and her son were going to eat their last meal and die. *Numbers 17:12 And she said, As the Lord thy God liveth, I have not a cake, but an handful of meal in a barrel, and a little oil in a cruse: and, behold, I am gathering two sticks, that I may go in and dress it for me and my son, that we may eat it, and die.*

Just as deception does not appear as deception, light often does not appear as light. Elijah, a true prophet of God, comes in: 13 But Elijah said to her, "Don't be afraid! Go ahead and do just what you've said, but make a little bread for me first. Then use what's left to prepare a meal for yourself and your son. *14 For this is what the Lord, the God of Israel, says: There will always be flour and olive oil left in your containers until the time when the Lord sends rain and the crops grow again!" 15 So she did as Elijah said, and she and Elijah and her family continued to eat for many days. 16 There was always enough flour and olive oil left in the containers, just as the Lord had promised through Elijah. 17 Some time later the woman's son became sick. He grew worse and worse, and finally he died. 18 Then she said to Elijah, "O man of God, what have you done to me? Have you come here to point out my sins and kill my son?" 19 But Elijah replied, "Give me your son." And he took the child's body from her arms, carried him up the stairs to the room where he was staying, and laid the body on his bed. 20 Then Elijah cried out to the Lord, "O Lord my God, why have you brought tragedy to this widow who has opened her home to me, causing her son to die?" 21 And he stretched himself out over the child three times and cried out to the Lord, "O Lord my God, please let this child's life return to him." 22 The Lord heard Elijah's prayer, and the life of the child returned, and he revived! 23 Then Elijah brought him down from the upper room and gave him to his mother. "Look!" he said. "Your son is alive!"*

If you have been predestined to live, God will intervene on your planned journey to die. This woman had lost her husband and was left alone with her son during a famine. You can imagine how dim her light had gotten. She could not control the circumstances and now her son has died. When lights are dim, not only is your sight off but your hearing is as well. In the depths of your heart where hope had all but faded, just when you least anticipated a glimmer of testimony, God will dispatch a resounding message to you. And that singular word has the power to revolutionize every facet of your existence. The voice of God is saying "Fear not, I'm doing a new thing in your life". Whether this word is a fresh revelation or a poignant reminder of God's prior declarations over your life, hear this: if you seize hold of this word and step forward with unwavering obedience, prepare yourself to be swept into the realm of supernatural possibilities beyond imagination. God inquired of me: "Do you grasp the weight of living a falsehood? Of favoring the crowd's consensus over your divine calling?" Understand this, anything falling short of God's grand design for your existence is not merely a fabrication; it's a blueprint leading to eventual demise.

Within the sacred realm of obedience, grace abounds, and divine strength courses through every fiber of your being. It became vividly clear to me that the path God summoned me to tread wasn't solely about stepping into certain shoes, roles, or paths alone, but with the essence of God Himself. As I fully embraced God's call and His plan for my life, I experienced a profound and almost otherworldly grace that transformed my journey into something truly awe-inspiring and supernatural. This revealed my dependence on God. I experienced such a sweet, supernatural grace in my life when I became willing to align with God and commit to what God said about me. There are parts of you that must go away so that the greater may arise. They must die, they must be crucified. There are parts of you that must fade away so that the true you can be present. You will never reach various realms in your current state. Jesus understood that to fulfill his purpose he had to die. But if he did many would live, *I John 7:14*. Understand that when you die from the pressure of needing validation of others, not only will you live but God will give you a light and a word that will cause others to transform and walk out their purpose and destiny. You have a mandate and have been trusted with a divine mission to transmit truth and blessings to the next generation.

In the realm of relationships, there are moments when our

paths must intersect to ignite brighter flames. There were many years when you yearned for others to witness your true essence, but God concealed it to safeguard your well-being. You found yourself with individuals who failed to appreciate your worth, and you implored them to recognize your value. They mistreated you, and you beseeched God to grant them the wisdom to treat you with greater respect. However, God refused because acquiescing would have meant compromising your entire life for subpar treatment, and His plans for you are vast. You are a blessing intended for a specific person. As you mature and release anxiety and fear, God will unveil incredible revelations to you. You are not an item up for auction, awaiting someone to bid on you. You are not a woman yearning to be discovered or seen; you are already found and seen. God wove you into your future husband's spirit from the very foundation of the world. He carries you in his spirit even now, and sooner rather than later, your paths will intersect, bringing to fruition what God designed from the beginning. The same principle applies to men—your future wives carry you in their spirits, praying fervently. They pray for your strength, courage, hope, protection, and love to fulfill God's ordained plan. Do not allow fear to govern the remainder of your life. When God brings something or someone to you, it becomes the collective responsibility of all parties involved to nurture, protect, and cultivate it, especially if He reunites something or someone in your life. God is the mastermind behind the greatest love stories ever told. The ball is in your court;

do not mishandle or lose it this time, for you may not receive another chance.

At times you wonder if I leave this toxic relationship will there be someone on the other side for me? If I relocate, will I have a support group? If I leave this job for what God is calling me to, will he sustain me? The answer is a resounding "Yes" to it all. God is not calling you to walk alone; He's calling you to walk in Him. I had to make a choice daily not to return to places or people that God had delivered me from, I experienced a form of strength through grace that allowed me to transcend and prevail over every weapon that formed. Because I chose God every time, the weapon could not prosper. I chose to speak what God said in every situation. Once you learn your purpose in life, you recognize your light and become empowered by it. It is at this moment that you realize that you are carrying a torch that must be passed on to generations. You now understand that the torch will shine and produce authentic light and life for you and generations to come throughout the nations. Having come to acknowledge the brilliance within you by God, you now have the strength to wield it. Take up the torch and pass on the flame!

Chapter 5 – She Found Me

"The two most important days in a person's life is the day you were born and the day you discover why." – Myles Munroe

This chapter elicited the most tears from me as I composed it, but they were tears filled with a profound sense of emotion. They were tears of awakening; a cathartic release that left me forever changed. As I neared the age of 45, a deep sensation of incompleteness began to wash over me. This feeling couldn't be dispelled through work or distractions; it was as if I had unconsciously started reaching for something elusive yet vital. Nevertheless, I remained baffled as to its nature. Throughout my life, I was frequently reminded that I possessed a pleasing appearance, a reasonably appealing physique, and a genuinely humble demeanor. Nonetheless, the only aspect I could truly perceive was my humility.

A SECOND CHANCE AT LIFE

My daughter, Kenneshia said Mom, I want you to do a photo shoot for your 45th birthday. I said OK. Not really thinking much about it. I thought we were just going to get pictures done right quick and go eat but she made it an entire event. An event that was all about me. Things were never really all about me. I was always lifting someone else up, validating someone else, motivating someone else, praying for someone else. She said Mom you must get a facial, your manicure and pedicure done. I'm remembering THAT FEELING. I couldn't describe it at the time, but later I could put words to what I was feeling. I was coming into womanhood. Womanhood at 45! Yes, at 45 I was still discovering who I was. As a young person, I had to look after my younger siblings, being a teenage Mom at 17 and married at 24. I've never had much time to myself. She booked the photo shoot a few days before my birthday. I got my manicure and pedicure done the day before my photo shoot. The morning of my photo shoot, I went to get a facial. I found myself seated there, utterly amazed. I was receiving a facial treatment, and the experience was incredibly soothing. The makeup artist was exceptional, and the ambiance was just right. While she pampered my face, there were moments when I felt transported to a different realm, if only for a brief time. When the photo proofs came back, I was blown away. I stared at an absolutely gorgeous woman. I was in awe of her beauty; her grace felt almost unattainable. It resembled one of those instances you'd find in a Sarah Jakes Roberts anecdote, where an image seemed to whisper, "Hey you," but took it a step further, proclaiming, "Hey you, you are me." At this juncture of my journey, I find myself fully immersed in the process of self-discovery.

When a person goes missing, it sparks an immediate concern: Where was the person last spotted? Alongside this, a flurry of inquiries emerges: Were they accompanied by someone? What attire did they have on? Who was their last companion? In which direction were they headed? It becomes vital to scan their recent social media updates. And amidst all this, one wonders: Were there any lingering worries on the missing person's mind? They meticulously search for any signs that could yield clues regarding the person's whereabouts. Let's delve deeper into one specific query: When was the person last SEEN?

Join me in this visualization: Take a mirror, gaze at your reflection, and pose this heartfelt question to yourself, "When was the last time I was TRULY SEEN?" Not the semblance that's merely projected? Not through the lens of motherhood? Not through the prism of fatherhood? Not defined by a role or a social media persona? Not just the caregiver version of you. The version of you whom God created from the foundation of the world. Your genuine and unadulterated self. Do you even remember her or him? For some, you can truly say I can finally see ME! Some are still missing. For others, you have never met your real self? It is almost impossible for you to see yourself without knowing who God is and developing a relationship with Him. The scripture says that when I am weak, I am strong. Numerous years went by during which I remained blind to my essence, preoccupied with safeguarding the persona others had constructed. I found myself defending a defined role. It was during those moments of vulnerability, or even illness, that instances of divine revelation would provide me fleeting glimpses of my authentic self.

For many individuals, the journey to liberation from diverse systems and patterns often involves navigating through intense challenges, ultimately leading to a profound understanding of one's true identity or should I say you will have gone through Hell. The majority of these frameworks possess a controlling, malevolent essence and are designed in manners that impose constraints upon you. Ranging from governmental and educational structures to societal norms, generational influences, traditional conventions, cultural paradigms, and diverse religious convictions, all of these can be recognized as systematic influences.

You must remain focused, intentional, and prayerful. Numerous individuals succumbed to these systems and never managed to break free. They are still STUCK or in the grave. We need not actively search for these systems; rather, they find us and are introduced to us from the moment we enter this world. We are inundated with them. We must remember *Matthew 6:33: But seek ye first the kingdom of God and His righteousness and all other things shall be added.* As humans, we go through life trying to find our true identity through broken systems. This, in turn, causes our concepts, ideas, and understanding of life and purpose to be inaccurate and altered, which leaves you even more thirsty for something real and meaningful. Total reliance on carnal systems causes you to be imprisoned in your mind, which in turn affects your decisions, abilities, and possibilities.

The place I often recall during tough times is my first apartment. In those days, I was young and determined to provide the best life for my daughter. We moved in when I was 19 years old on the Southside of Birmingham, with a view over the city. It marked the beginning of my adulthood, coupled with the responsibility of raising a child. In that apartment, we prayed for protection and guidance, experiencing peace, love, and joy. Kenneshia and I would snuggle in bed with popcorn and juice, watching our two favorite movies, "Beauty and the Beast" and "Fox and the Hound."

During challenging moments, my mind would return to that place of solitude. Unlike reminiscing about a person from the past or longing for a previous good phase in life, this time was different. I didn't go looking for something or someone, it came looking for me. The "She" in She Found Me is my soul. It was like the doorbell rang and there stood my soul looking at me. I'm standing there in awe looking at her and she is just as much in awe looking back at me. It was as if time stood still. There was like an alas, I have finally found my resting place. It was the greatest, most special reunion I had ever experienced. Imagine having a child that went missing and was found. It's as though my very soul had been abandoned and replaced by an unfamiliar identity. Alternatively, envision stumbling upon a hidden sibling or child you never knew existed. The electrifying instances of reconnection hold the power to completely astonish. She found me but old reflections, old mindsets, and delusional spirits would still vex me. I constantly had to renew my mind. Now that she's here, I had to learn how to know, love, protect, and give her the rest she needed. I had to learn to be attentive to her needs. She was this beautiful, confident, selfless, brown woman who I adored. I would look at myself in the mirror and say you are so beautiful. I love your skin, your dimples, and your hair but most of all I love your heart. It's so big and compassionate. I was learning to embrace me, not who society made me, not who the church made me but who God made me. I finally realized that I was complete. Everything I was looking for on the outside was already in me. I fell in love with DESTINY. I began to claim it, reach for it, and embrace it. I knew God had a well-thought-out plan when He created me. He had already accounted for every mistake I would make. He knew the level of grace and mercy I would need. He knew that one day I would SEE and embrace this wonderful creation whose earthly name was Charlotte.

One day I lay in bed, feeling like I was about to die. I was in pain, my energy was gone, I was lethargic, it was horrible. My then-husband at the time came into the room and he was listening to a woman teaching the word of God. Her voice was so anointed and carried healing in it. I could barely talk, so I tapped on the headboard to get his attention. I said, remember that lady you are listening to, I want to listen to her when I feel better. He gave me the strangest look, said okay, and walked out of the room. The next day when I was feeling better. I said who was the lady you were listening to. He looked at me strangely again and said that was you. I said what!?!? He said that was you and proceeded to bring back my remembrance of the message. I said pull it back up so I can hear it again. I sat down and said I am that powerful woman of God. I was in awe. I listened to the entire message and was extremely blessed by it. I found it difficult, at times, to maintain that feeling, to embrace my identity, and to own who I was. However, as time passed, I held to my true self so tightly that the thought of separating from her or turning back made me nauseous. The desolation I once felt had turned into a resolution. I had come to a season of resolve with a mind and vigorous spirit like Esther. I declared that I was called to the kingdom for a time such as this and if I perish, I perish – *Esther 4:16.* Nothing can be compared when you discover who you are, learn to love yourself, and embrace her or him wholeheartedly. I learned that in some seasons of my life, I was better for myself by myself. You realize everything you will ever need is tied to your destiny, so you focus on it. Dr. Myles Munroe once said, "The greatest mystery in life is that your destiny was chosen by God but its fulfillment is decided by you". Stop your mind from traveling in reverse. You are a complete work but you must accept that fact and truth. You are one decision away from a whole, new season in your life.

Chapter 6 – You Don't Need Permission to Live

You are responsible for your life. You can't keep blaming some-body else for your dysfunction. Life is really about moving on.
-Oprah Winfrey

YOU DON'T NEED PERMISSION TO LIVE! If you're stuck in a situation where someone is trying to control you, you might end up falling for their lies and fears. In the process, you end up missing out on what you're really meant to do in life. It took me an additional two years to fully comprehend the significance of my grand-daughter Kennedi's statement: YOU DON'T NEED PERMIS-SION TO LIVE. She was saying that I am responsible and accountable for how I live my life. The "seeing" eyes of my eight-year-old granddaughter not only had natural sight but spiritual sight also. God used Kennedi to speak into my present life and future. She changed the trajectory of my life while canceling the assignment of the enemy. Those words would live in the walls of my home, take root in my mind, and echo in the chambers of my heart. They provided solace, whispered to me in the midnight silence, and stood as my defender when the enemy attempted to snatch away my joy. In this season I released fear and surrendered to God. It was like a car that ran out of gas. I was delivered from the control of others. It was where God wanted me and where I wanted to be. I had finally come to a place of silence. There was stillness, a hush, no outside noise or interference, I had entered the holy place. There was no concern about who I hadn't connected with, and the ringing phone was no longer a source of worry. It felt like my world had paused, granting me the space to breathe freely—the air of a new beginning, a fresh start, and a profound connection with God. The need for validation from others was fading away. Despite the love I had for those urging me to come here or there, the voice of the One who created me resonated louder and more powerfully than any of them. I couldn't bring myself to call and explain my whereabouts. I was exactly where I belonged—hidden in the secret place. *Psalms 91:1-2. He that dwelleth in the secret place of the most High shall abide under the shadow of the Almighty. I will say of the Lord, He is my refuge and my fortress: my God; in Him will I trust.* On this day, I repeatedly heard the chime of incoming Cash App notifications, the satisfying ping of invoices getting paid, and the rhythmic counting of dollar bills. I couldn't help but recognize the prophetic nature of these sounds. Gradually, those dollar bills seemed to transform into the gentle clinking of coins dropping. God said, this is your life, you are running out of time, your time is like currency, and you are running out of it. God knew I was trying to live in unfruitful seasons that He had ended. God let me know that I lived most of my life for others and I was about to run out of time on this journey. My fears centered around people, what they might say, think, or how my life would appear, became inconsequential. God was dismantling self-sabotaging behaviors, destiny-destroying cycles, and unbelief. *Matthew 22:14 Many are called but few are chosen.* I was aware of my calling for a significant purpose, yet I found myself deeply immersed in hurt, pain, and disappointments, risking the chance to experience the most pivotal moment in my life. Each day, I committed to trusting God and facilitating closure in my life. Certain doors needed closing, and some relationships had to be severed, but these actions were essential. I had to place my trust in the future that awaited me.

Philippians 3:13 Brethren, I count not myself to have apprehended: but this one thing I do, forgetting those things which are behind, and reaching forth unto those things which are before. Ephesians 1:11 In him we were also chosen,[a] having been predestined according to the plan of him who works out everything in conformity with the purpose of his will (NIV).

God let me know the only person standing in my way was me. It took years to understand the internal conflict. There was a battle between who I was and who God was calling me to be. There was no one else to blame. I didn't need permission from anyone, God was authoring a new life and there was no room for dysfunction. God began to describe grace to me as funding. Essentially, He conveyed a message of no more support or tolerance for dysfunction in my life. It's comparable to a child consistently wearing two left shoes; over time, the right foot adjusts to the left shoe, learning to walk upright until the discomfort fades. Similarly, when dysfunction becomes a familiar space, one becomes comfortable in it. During God's process of delivering and elevating you, He begins stripping away everything that lacks His characteristics. While God extends grace, He is not obligated to support our constant incorrect choices. When actions start colliding and jeopardizing destiny, the funding ceases, and a realignment becomes necessary. God didn't alter my situation; He transformed me. Just as you adapt to dysfunction, you must learn to adapt to wholeness.

I began to strengthen my emotional and mental skills. I initiated a practice of affirming positive words in my life and established personal goals. I delved into the source of my discomfort, it was because I was being required to feel, feel the moment, and embrace it. There were moments I would look in the mirror and ask myself is this real? I saw through a new set of lenses. Life was becoming more beautiful every day. No longer is there someone to point fingers at. You've faced mismanagement, mistreatment, abuse, neglect, and deception, yet God prevented it from being your downfall. Maya Angelou wrote a poem titled: "I Know Why The Caged Bird Sings". This poem speaks of hope and resilience during fearful times. Let this excerpt from the poem encourage you: *But a caged bird stands on the grave of dreams his shadow shouts on a nightmare scream his wings are clipped and his feet are tied so he opens his throat to sing.* Maintain your ability to speak life even in challenging times. Despite everything done to you, you opened your mouth and began to sing. Though your heart was broken, faith shattered, and dreams vanished, you chose to open your mouth and sing. You begin to degree "I don't know how God is going to do it, but I know He will bring me out". You sang in the darkness, giving God praise out of a hard place. It's in the dark places that you see the light more vividly. *John 1:5 And the light shineth in darkness; and the darkness comprehended it not.* You made the devil out of a liar and everyone on his team. God showed up for you and you will forever sing.

Staying in a controlling situation despite being delivered by God reflects dysfunction on your part. If you've made efforts to make someone recognize your worth, and they choose not to, it's because, for someone to treat you as the valuable person you are, they must confront the person they are not. Instead of questioning others about their treatment of you, it's crucial to ask yourself why you're treating yourself this way. Relying on others for permission to live diminishes your capabilities, hinders your personal growth, and leaves you in a state of uncertainty. Certain individuals may support you as long as you stay within the boundaries they've set for you. However, once you surpass their expectations, envy and resentment may surface. Take authority over your life and ensure you never relinquish control again. Giving people that kind of authority over your life can put you in jeopardy with God. Control and manipulation are forms of witchcraft and jealousy is as cruel as the grave. If you are in any form of relationship that exhibits such traits, sever ties with those relationships.

In *Judges 6*, God was instructing Gideon to rescue Israel. Gideon told God that his clan was the weakest in Manasseh, and he was the least in his father's house. God continued to strengthen Gideon and got the victory. Gideon didn't learn anything new, he just assessed what was already in him.

Having triumphed over self-doubt, it's now time to conquer other challenges. God's guidance doesn't instruct us to control people; rather, it emphasizes the importance of self-control, which is a gift from God. *Galatians 5:22-23 But the Holy Spirit produces this kind of fruit in our lives: love, joy, peace, patience, kindness, goodness, faithfulness, [23] gentleness, and self-control.* Additionally, we are called to dominate over resources. Through God's guidance, we should pray and exert influence over the seven mountains: Family, Religion, Business, Politics, Education, Media, and Arts praying *Matthew 6:10 Your kingdom come, your will be done, on earth as it is in heaven.*

On several occasions, God would tell me that the wine is ready, but the skin cannot sustain this new wine (*Luke 5:36-38*). In other words, I am ready to fill you and present you with destiny, but you are not ready. Dysfunctional environments can cause you to be jaded. You still have the old mindset; you are still riddled with fear and people's opinions rather than God's word. I had been jaded by my present environment. However, I was finally back at a place of faith and trust in God, where I had to wait for His directions for every step I took. This was so frightening to me, prompting me to ensure all my affairs were in order. I made sure all the life policies and accounts were in place. Uncertain of what lay ahead, the only certainty was that I stood on the brink of a journey, and this phase of my life would soon be behind me. Living doesn't require permission, but it also doesn't grant permission to alter the life God has predestined for you. This marks a transition from God's permissive will to His perfect will. Remember the outcome is not based on how they change, but how you change.

Chapter 7 – The Perfect Storm

Traveling through life, braving its seas, and one day you realize that you are in a perfect storm. You often hear about the storms of life but being at the mercy of a perfect storm, you realize there's a chance you will lose it all, even your life. I was at the point in my life that I knew the only way to survive this particular storm was through death. Undoubtedly, this phase marked the most challenging period in my life. I exhausted every effort in trying to mend, patch, and conceal my hurt and wounds. I temporarily took depression medication and poured all I could into my work. Counseling was a resource I fully tapped into. Typically, a prayer or a word of encouragement would provide sustenance for an extended period. However, this time, the storm was not letting me out. It raged fiercely, marking a battle waged between the forces of light and darkness, life and death. Nothing seemed to fortify me, except my willingness to surrender. I was hemorrhaging out joy, peace, trust, hope, sanity, everything. I could no longer hide it. It showed on my face, spirit, actions, and health. In the film The Perfect Storm, the crew expended every available effort to battle the tempest, only to find themselves trapped in the heart of a perilous and catastrophic storm. The boat had taken a great beating from the winds and waves. There would be moments of celebration and optimism only to see that they had not beaten the storm. In various instances throughout my marriage, I put in significant effort, only to recognize that during specific periods, I found myself contending with challenges in solitude. No matter how diligently I tried to cover the pain, it would still seep through the bandages. I was at a place where I was forced to stop fighting. I was forced to surrender. It was like I was forced to become one with the storm. I was forced into riding its tumultuous waves, feeling its intensity, witnessing its fury, and desperately attempting to comprehend it. The Perfect Storm was based on a true story and my life almost mirrored it. To look at the intense moments of the crew being stuck in the storm was heartbreaking, the strong winds and waves battered the boat and everyone on it. It's still unclear exactly what became of the Andrea Gail and its crew. The crew perished and many details are a matter of speculation. No distress signals were ever sent, very little wreckage was ever found and there were no survivors to interview or remains to examine. The boat and crew members were never found, and all died at sea. The sole factors that prevented my fate from resembling that of those aboard the Andrea Gail were my faith in God and my determination to transmit distress signals. I was determined not to leave behind shattered, unidentifiable wreckage, debris, and rubbish as my legacy. The thought of allowing the sea to engulf me and succumb in such a manner was not an option. Suffering in silence was no longer acceptable. Ending my life in such a way was out of the question. I was resolute in not letting anyone wonder about my fate. We are often instructed to hide our pain, hurt, and struggles, to refrain from discussing them, and simply rely on prayer. God placed family and a small group of friends to help me, they heard and saw my distress. They loved, cared, and prayed for me and helped keep the taste of life in my mouth. A crucial thing to remember is that when the crew on the Andrea Gail lost signal, they could not call out and no one could call in; leaving them at the mercy of the storm.

I can't imagine the number of people who have committed suicide because they felt they could not tell anyone what they were going through. Society, along with certain members of religious communities, has pushed many individuals into a state of self-sabotage, self-destructive behavior, false guilt, and in some tragic cases, even death. There were moments when I pleaded with God to summon me home and welcome me into heaven. In those times, I would engage in self-dialogue, reminding myself that I've never been one to cheat, so why start now? It would be morally wrong to cheat myself out of life, to cheat God, my family, my assignment, and the generations to come. Why forfeit the opportunity to be a voice for those who didn't make it, those who carried their stories to the grave? Storms often drive people into isolation.

One might wonder what led me to finally seek help. It wasn't a single, decisive moment but rather the cumulative weight of profound hurts that was dragging me down, a state of pure desperation. I recognized that if I endured another significant setback, recovery might be beyond reach. Several weeks later, I sent a text to a dear friend. My pain was so overwhelming that I couldn't wait for her to respond via text, so I decided to give her a call. However, when she picked up and greeted me, I found myself unable to speak; instead, all I could do was sob inconsolably. After she prayed for me, she talked to me in a manner in which I've never heard her speak, she said these words to me: "FIGHT LIKE HELL!" She said, Charlotte "FIGHT LIKE HELL" for your life. Do you hear me? "FIGHT LIKE HELL!" "FIGHT LIKE HELL" for your children and grandchildren. "FIGHT LIKE HELL!" You have fought for so many others, it's time for you to "FIGHT LIKE HELL" for yourself. Her words cut deep as she warned me that remaining in certain cycles could lead to a point of no return, a place from which recovery might be impossible. Her concern touched my soul, and I couldn't help but cry even harder. She asked, "Can I reach out to Kenneshia?" Reluctantly, I replied, "Yes, go ahead and call her." There were times when I attempted to shield Kenneshia from witnessing my moments of brokenness. Although she did, I didn't want her to carry the burden of my pain and suffering. After ending the call with my friend, I activated the camera on my phone and gazed at my tear-streaked face, overwhelmed with sobs, and my nose running and said to myself, Charlotte "FIGHT LIKE HELL", "FIGHT LIKE HELL", "FIGHT LIKE HELL!" However, my boat (representing my soul) had weathered such relentless battering from the storms of life and this connection that I discovered myself incapable of returning to shore without assistance. All I needed was a gentle tow, a patient guiding hand. Avoid jerking me, snatching me, or moving too swiftly. Love me back to shore and remain by my side. Exercise patience with me; if I require a break, halt the towing. When I seek moments alone, pause the towing. And when I need to rest and shed a few more tears, kindly stop the towing. It's in these pauses that my strength will rebuild, and the journey will become more bearable.

I said Charlotte, "I love you, and God loves you too." Unfortunately, I didn't have any Kleenex to wipe away my tears, so I had to make do with the shirt I was wearing, doing my best to dry my face. There's a unique intensity in looking at your reflection and witnessing the pain etched in your eyes, the evidence of your brokenness, and the scars on your battered soul. It's a stark reminder of how fear and the influence of others have, at times, robbed you of precious moments in life. Yet, in that reflection, I didn't just see despair, I also saw courage, hope, truth, faith, love, and the strength to declare that there is a life waiting beyond the current struggle. I reassured myself that this was the last time I would allow myself to be in such a condition, making a solemn promise to trust in what God had already revealed to me. It was a battle be-tween the old me, still wrestling with the new me, the version that God had predestined for me.

It was a collision of mindsets, the old mind against the re-newed mind. The mere thought of divorce made me profoundly uncomfortable, just hearing the word made me nauseous. Not to mention I struggled with understanding grace. Various church set-tings and the experiences gained in my personal history ingrained in me the belief that any minor mistake I made would lead me to damnation. Consequently, I dedicated significant effort to ensure that I never erred, which was impossible. During that period, I felt as though God was constantly watching, ready to condemn me to hell at the slightest misstep. I am truly grateful for the transfor-mation of my mindset in this regard. Some journeys I did not want to take or be a part of my story due to the pain of it. However, He quickly reminded me that He is the author and finisher of my faith. He shared that the person who had endured molestation was ada-mant about excluding that painful chapter from their life story. The individual who faced the heart-wrenching experience of a stillborn baby wished to shield that sorrowful moment from becoming a permanent part of their narrative. Another soul, who navigated a harrowing journey through abusive foster care, fervently desired to keep those dark memories out of their life's tale. The widower, grappling with the profound grief of losing a spouse, longed to pre-serve the memory of their love without the overshadowing pain of that loss. Similarly, the one subjected to both verbal and physical abuse fervently wished to erase those traumatic imprints from the pages of their life story, and the list extended. Each person hopes to navigate past the shadows of their past and script a narrative that reflects strength and resilience. God said, I will restore years that were stolen back to you (Joel 2:25). I got quiet and started worshiping God, pouring out sincere praise of worship, gratitude, and thanksgiving. *Ephesians 6:12 For we wrestle not against flesh and blood, but against principalities, against powers, against the rulers of the darkness of this world, against spiritual wickedness in high places.*

Life is not an audition, it's a predestined journey. We don't have the privilege of selecting or auditioning for specific roles in this grand narrative. There are no roles where we're always the hero, universally beloved, or where every tale concludes with happiness. We don't have the authority to craft the storyline or even name the overarching movie. However, what we do have is the opportunity for a second chance to align with His original plan for our lives. We have the chance to become whole, to heal, and to unveil our true selves. We can embark on a journey of self-discovery and recovery. We're allowed to narrate our own unique story, to experience giving love once more, and to be loved in return. Ultimately, we have the chance to fulfill our purpose and destiny.

Similarly, to the crew of the Andrea Gail in The Perfect Storm, we underestimate the warnings and conditions; many times, personal storms arise because one tends to ignore the warning signs and refuse to acknowledge reality, so in turn we close our hearts to

Godly divine guidance. In my younger years, I used to say, "If someone had to suffer, let it be me." Little did I know that I was setting myself up for significant pain, emotional distress, and mental unrest. The collapse I experienced was due to issues like control, one-sided perspectives, lack of accountability, and mismanagement, none of which were my own doing. In a sense, my upbringing had primed me for a scenario like this but also prepared me to overcome it. As mentioned earlier, I had been guided into specific roles throughout my life, and the events described in the chapter titled "It's Time to Dig Deep and Uncover" molded me for relationships of authority. While I had learned the significance of personal accountability, there was no instruction on holding others accountable. Moreover, I had been conditioned to adapt to the expectations and behaviors of others, even when they were unhealthy or detrimental. At times, the echoes of individuals and circumstances that once sought to dismantle you and crush your spirit still reverberate. Though those people may no longer be part of your life, the impact of their actions, deeds, and hurtful words lingers within the walls of your heart and mind, threatening to infiltrate your new season. To overcome this, you must exercise the authority bestowed upon you by God to silence the negativity that surrounds you.

Often, we try to help God as Sarah did in *Genesis 16-18 because of unbelief.* God promised Abraham and Sarah a son in their old age. Sarah was childless until she was 90 years old. Because they looked at their current state, they attempted to assist God by having Sarah's handmaid sleep with Abraham creating Ishmael. Regardless of what you create in your endeavor to assist God, God will ultimately demand your obedience to His original promise, which in their case was Isaac. Abraham and Sarah were predestined to be the father and mother of many nations. Isaac was the promised child, and God's divine plan remained unchanged. The birth of Ismael never replaced the plan of God. God returned thirteen years later to confirm that the covenant blessing would come through Isaac, not Ismael. Abraham and Sarah gave birth in their old age just as God had ordained. At some point, God will require your full obedience to His perfect will, regardless of the length of time you spent in His permissive will. This indicates that God will come back into your life, and regardless of how much time has elapsed, He will realign you to be in accordance with His perfect will. It might take many years, but the promised outcome will endure. When a storm arises in your life, its purpose isn't to annihilate you; rather, it's there to reposition you for the blessing. Repositioning might involve closing doors you opened, severing relationships, and summoning the courage to enter a new season of your life.

During certain life journeys, there will be individuals who are unable to recognize and appreciate the genuine and beautiful blessing that you represent. Their own insecurities and negative inclinations may obscure their vision. Nevertheless, there comes a moment when God's message, much like the words spoken by my eight-year-old granddaughter, will resonate within you: "You don't require anyone's permission to embrace life." Life often unfolds cyclically, almost as if it follows a complete 360-degree path. This journey may at times seem like you've ventured outwards only to return empty-handed, but that perspective warrants reconsideration. In truth, it's a testament to God's favor and blessings upon you. Many have embarked on diverse journeys but never found their way back, yet you stand as a testament to God's unwavering plan. You've traversed the depths of your plans and desires, and now you've arrived at the very path God preordained for you. This is cause for celebration and praise. If you feel that a past situation has left you with less than you deserved, surrender it to God. Watch in awe as He transforms your life into something remarkable and fulfilling. Remember, this isn't the end but rather the beginning of a new chapter, one in which God's purpose unfolds in magnificent ways beyond imagination. Allow learned lessons to turn into blessings. Even though you've been through the storm and rain, you survived it. You don't look like what you've been through. Victory is yours. Celebrate life!

Chapter 8 - It's Nice to Meet You

When starting a new journey or ending an old journey, never forget why you did it.
-Charlotte Ford

As I gaze into the mirror, I warmly greet the person staring back at me. It's a moment of profound connection, where I perceive a glimpse of what I believe to be the divine blueprint that God has woven into the tapestry of my existence. In that mirrored image, I discern the intricate threads of purpose and destiny, as if God's master plan for my life is laid bare before me. This encounter with my reflection becomes a sacred affirmation, a reminder that I am on a path meticulously designed by a higher power. It's a recognition of the unique qualities, talents, and potential that have been bestowed upon me, each serving as a piece of the intricate puzzle that is my life's purpose.

With each passing day, I strive to align my actions, decisions, and aspirations with this divine plan, understanding that I am a co-creator in the ongoing narrative of my life. So, as I exchange this heartfelt greeting with myself in the mirror, it's not just a casual introduction; it's a profound acknowledgment of the remarkable journey I am on, guided by the hand of God. In this reflection, I perceive an awakened soul, a vibrant spirit, and a beautiful, confident woman of God. It's as if I'm witnessing the embodiment of His divine plan. I see more than just an individual; I see boundless possibilities and hope that can span generations and impact nations. I sense the presence of those who tragically perished without the chance to share their stories, their spirits lingering in this sacred reflection. Moreover, I see the potential to ignite the lights of countless souls who will find inspiration within the pages of this book, each possessing their unique talents and gifts waiting to be uncovered. I embody strength, structure, and authority, a testament to God's declaration: "Let us make man in our image, after our likeness: and let them have dominion over the fish of the sea, and over the fowl of the air, and the cattle, and all the earth, and over every creeping thing that creepeth upon the earth." This introspective moment is not merely a superficial encounter with my image; it's a profound communion with God, a revelation of the purpose and potential that God has lovingly woven into the fabric of my being.

To every woman who departed from this earthly realm prematurely, I carry the echoes of your voices within my own. To those who endured the heavy yoke of slavery, to those who suffered at the hands of abusers, to those who were ensnared in the web of narcissists, and to those who bore their pain in silence, I stand in solidarity with you. To every woman who was coerced into becoming someone else's shadow, to those confined within prison walls, to the girls and women who fell prey to the dark world of human trafficking, and to the teenage mothers who faced unfathomable challenges, your stories resonate deeply within my heart. For every woman who lost the ability to feel emotions and for every girl and woman who endured the traumatic scars of childhood molestation, your unseen struggles are etched in the corners of my soul, even if your narratives remain untold.

Each time I find my voice to share my journey, I do so with your indomitable spirits in my heart, a chorus of resilience that transcends time. I recognize that I can stand and tell my story today because of the brave souls who walked this path before me and found the strength to stand tall. In this awakening, God has granted me a new lease on life, one intricately woven with the original purpose and plan He envisioned for me. I am filled with an insatiable hunger for truth, a reclamation of my voice, the pursuit of sacred dreams, the embrace of covenant sisterhood, and a life that far surpasses any vision I could have conjured on my own.

When I extend the greeting, "It's nice to meet you," to the reflection in the mirror, it is equally an affirmation that it's beautiful to meet us all. We are interconnected, regardless of the diverse routes we've traversed. Although I penned this book, it was a collective effort; each of you guided me on wings of courage and resilience. I represent you, and you represent me. We form a sister-hood destined to grow in strength, power, unity, and hope. We stand as a testament to the resilience of the human spirit, and our stories will be a beacon of light for those who seek solace and inspiration in the face of adversity. As I stand before the mirror, I utter those powerful words to myself: "It's a pleasure to meet you, and I vow never to lose sight of you again." These words carry the weight of our earlier discussions, where we delved into the phases of uncovering, discovering, and recovering. With the grace I've been granted to recover and begin anew, my heart brims with emotion. I can now confidently declare that experiencing my true self, acknowledging my existence, and feeling the essence of my being is an incomparable joy. What gazes back at me from the mirror is a testament to grace, humility, gratitude, and love.

To all those who will find hope and inspiration in my story, I reiterate: that while I may have put pen to paper, this narrative is a collective endeavor. We wrote it together, as life itself is a series of journeys, each marked by both endings and new beginnings. Stubbornly clinging to a season that has run its course can be detrimental. Every journey, with its unique challenges and revelations, unveils a piece of your true self. Some revelations may signal the need for certain aspects to wither away, while others call for a reawakening. I encourage you to take notes in every season, for some destinations are best left behind, as they no longer have a place in your evolving narrative. You perceive yourself differently because you have become different. Everything about you has evolved. In a remarkable shift, you made choices that placed yourself, God, purpose, destiny, and love at the forefront.

In that reflection, you see God – the embodiment of love. You believed in the boundless love of God, trusting that if He spoke it, He would manifest it. We stand as living proof of that divine performance. God has allowed every phase of my life from my upbringing, previous marriage, and a mirage of experiences to work out for my good. To adversity, rejection, and pain, I extend gratitude for the lessons they imparted on this journey, but you also bid them farewell collectively. In the mirror of my newfound self, I see resilience, faith, and a testament to the transformative power of unwavering belief.

Brianna Wiest says, *"Your new life is going to cost you your old one. It's going to cost you your comfort zone and your sense of direction. It's going to cost you relationships and friends. It's going to cost you being liked and understood. It doesn't matter. The people who are meant for you are going to meet you on the other side. You're going to build a new comfort zone around the things that move you forward. Instead of being liked, you're going to be loved. Instead of being understood, you're going to be seen. All you're going to lose is what was built for a person you no longer are."*

I say to you again as Jesus said to the damsel in *Mark 1:31, Talitha cumi - Arise! Arise! Arise!* Feed your greatest hunger, receive the energy you have released, and silence the triggers of your painful past. Healing is a journey. It's time to live. You have a second chance at life!

About The Author

As we come to the closing of the book, "A Second Chance at Life," we delve into the life and remarkable journey of Charlotte Ford, a native of Birmingham, Alabama, and the cherished daughter of Earnestine Ford. Her profound love extends to her three remarkable children, Kenneshia, John, and Joshua, and her two precious grandchildren, Kennedi and Khi.

Charlotte's multifaceted identity encompasses her role as a licensed and ordained Pastor, bringing with her a wealth of leadership experience. She is not only a motivational speaker and prayer intercessor but also a dedicated entrepreneur. Her unwavering commitment lies in the realms of women's and children's ministry, a passion that resonates deeply within her heart. Charlotte guides and supports women as they embark on the journey of discovering and rediscovering their God-given identities, stressing the importance of alignment within the Kingdom of God.

Beyond her spiritual calling, Charlotte has also earned a Master of Business Administration and assumes the role of CEO at Balloon Studio and More LLC. She thrives in a professional leadership position within Human Resources. Her name, Charlotte, carries connotations of royalty and originates from French or Italian, meaning freedom.

Having embarked on her transformative journey towards self-healing and fostering an authentic relationship with God, Charlotte's aspiration is to touch the lives of countless individuals with messages of hope, empowerment, and love. She stands resolute in her belief that, regardless of life's trials, tribulations, and suffering, a brighter tomorrow always awaits.

Made in the USA
Columbia, SC
02 December 2023

27051352R10059